YOU CAN BE YOUR OWN SEX THERAPIST

by CAROLE ALTMAN, Ph.d.

A Systematized Behavioral Approach to
Enhancing Your Sensual Pleasures
Improving Your Sexual Enjoyment
Curing Sexual Dysfunctions

D1316380

Published by
CASPER PUBLISHING

To my children who have faith in me
To Rick - my inspiration and my love
To the hundreds of men and women
who helped me to realize -
"You Can Be Your Own Sex Therapist."

CONTENTS

Section I

YOU CAN
BE YOUR OWN
SEX THERAPIST
Concepts and Procedures

Chapter I

Why Do-It-Yourself Sex Therapy Can Work for You

THE ORGASM. The physiological response of the body to a variety of physical stimulations, the orgasm. The transcendence of all. The sharing of loving feelings in a giving and taking of energy and excitement, the orgasm. A circular flow which has no equal. A moment in space and time during which we are completely released—no tensions, no worries, no fears . . . the orgasm. The phenomenon most misunderstood and most discussed, the orgasm. We all want it. We all need it. We all seek it.

Unfortunately, however, there are those who find it difficult to fully enjoy their sexual lives. Those who suffer from a sexual inadequacy or from inhibitions which deprive them of their right to pleasure. Sex therapy is the answer for them. Sex therapy is so well-defined, so systematized, so simple to follow and so easy to effect that patients can work on their own, following step-by-step procedures.

You can do it yourself.

I have been working as a psychotherapist for over seven years. At first, I followed all of the psychotherapeutic techniques I was trained in during over 500 hours of extensive experience and supervision. These included bioenergetic and Gestalt approaches, as well as sensitivity training and encounter work.

But I experienced a great deal of frustration as a therapist. I observed patients struggling for months at a time with very

3

little visible gain. Of course change is difficult, even with therapy, and so I struggled along with the patients, my frustrations empathic with theirs.

Many of my patients were suffering from sexual hang-ups. Working with these patients, I observed that personal growth and change were achieved with relative ease once such hang-ups were resolved.

For example, a young woman I'll call Jan, who was having a terrible problem with her identity—unsure of whether she wanted to stay married or not, unsure of her career, unsure of the direction her life had taken—was also unable to achieve orgasm. We began using the techniques you'll read about in this book to ameliorate the problem. She followed the directions and exercises without any therapeutic discussion as to *why* she couldn't achieve orgasm.

Within two weeks Jan was able to have an orgasm through self-stimulation. After only three sessions, she and her husband were deeply involved in improving their sex life and were experiencing orgasm together, following the techniques described in this book.

The most gratifying thing was that not only did Jan's sex life improve but she was a happier, more contented person both in her work and in her marriage. In fact, two years have passed since then. Jan is now pregnant and very excited about her marriage and about becoming a mother.

Success in such cases motivated me to do more sex therapy with my patients. I studied all of the known techniques, but I also began developing my own approaches. By now my studies had showed me that the program I had worked out for Jan, for example, was original in that it offered much more than the traditional cure for nonorgasmic women. My approach was a fuller, more complete program than those that existed in the sex clinics I studied.

I geared my private practice to the specialty of sex therapy, seeing new patients only if they had specific sex problems they wanted solved. I led groups of couples with sexual problems; I discussed sexual problems on several radio programs on which I was a guest. My cable-TV program, "Awareness with Carole Altman," became directed more toward sexual problems. My guests were eminent authorities in the field: Dr.

Barbara Hogan of the Cornell Medical College Sex Clinic, Dr. Freyda Zell of the Consultation Center for Women, Dr. Barry Lubetkin of the Institute for Behavior Modification in New York, and others.

On the TV show, I interviewed couples who had resolved their sex problems using the program I was developing. I also offered advice and suggestions to people who called me about sexual problems. One of my case histories was discussed in a *New York Post* article on sex therapists.

I continued learning as much as I could about current sex therapy approaches and improving and adding to my own unique approach.

I was enjoying my work. Results in sex therapy are much more rapid than in the slower-moving therapies I was used to—and more dramatic. Sexual problems are often at the root of many other problems. Solve the one and you solve the other. You can imagine how gratifying it is for a therapist to watch a patient change from a frightened, insecure individual to a happy confident one.

With every such successful patient, I felt more and more confident in my approach to sex therapy.

I was constantly analyzing the process my patients went through. I realized more and more that I was merely a tool in the hands of my patients. They used me basically as a source of information. They improved, were cured, and became happier due largely to their own efforts and their own determination.

The techniques of sex therapy, developed first by Masters and Johnson, and further refined in hundreds of sex clinics throughout the United States, are all based on a sort of do-it-yourself approach. Patients with sexual problems are given directions which tell them what they should do. Then they go home and try to follow these directions. They discuss their attempts with the therapist, and the therapist then helps them over situations which were difficult for them and helps make it easier for them to follow the directions the next time.

For example, following traditional sex therapy, I might tell a couple to be kind to each other for one hour each evening. During their next session they might discuss with me the fact that he or she had trouble being "kind," and we would talk

about the difficulty of giving to each other, of receiving gra-
ciously, and of paying attention to each other in general.
Together, we would devise a plan which, hopefully, would
work better during the next week, and they would experience
less difficulty in being "kind" to each other.

I realized that patients could, actually, learn to have these
discussions on their own, follow directions, and work through
their own problems, without a therapist present, if they were
shown how in as simple and direct a way as possible.

This may sound "too easy" to many sex therapists, but I feel
strongly that this is what sex therapy should be, essentially,
where no other severe psychological problems are present.

I was more and more entranced with the idea of patients
becoming cured through their own effort and determination.
Seeing my patients improve so rapidly and easily, largely
through their own efforts, the idea of an effective program of
do-it-yourself sex therapy seemed more and more possible to
me.

I continued to develop my own sex therapy program,
encouraging my patients to do more and more of the work
themselves. By now, my schedule was becoming so full that I
could not possibly see everyone who called for an appointment. I began to give the exercises and techniques I was
developing to patients without even seeing them. I gave them
written instructions about what to do, and found that they
followed these with the same success as patients who did see
me.

I continued to give written instructions to those patients
who were willing to work with a help-yourself sex therapy
program. I monitored their experiences, constantly improving the program so that it could work for anyone, on his own,
without a therapist and at a very low cost.

The completed program took over two years to develop and
refine. I worked with over two hundred patients. I tested the
system with all new patients who were willing to be their own
sex therapists. There were many who welcomed the opportunity to work at home. Some lived far from my office and
found travel difficult; others could not afford the fees. Still
others welcomed the chance to avoid the embarrassment of
sharing their most intimate thoughts with a stranger—even a

therapist. Some liked the challenge of being on their own, working toward goals which they themselves set, at their own pace and in the privacy of their homes.

The reactions of my patients were encouraging and exciting. They realized that they could change a part of their lives by being determined, by caring enough about themselves to work hard and follow directions. They knew that *they* were responsible for their own success or failure with the kind of therapy I was offering and they accepted the challenge.

Some patients, of course, needed more encouragement than others. Some needed more individual attention at first before they could get started on help-yourself therapy. That was to be expected at that early stage, since the program had not been developed fully. But these snags have now been removed by the best teacher: experience. I have developed questionnaires and other devices to help you avoid the problems which arose in the early days of the program.

For example, some people needed guidance to define their problems and to focus on what they wanted from sex therapy. Not everyone is clear as to what their goals are. For such people, I have developed the questionnaire in Chapter 4, *And Now You Begin.*

I also devised the system of writing contracts, committing you to yourself and to your partner, clarifying exactly what you will do for yourselves and exactly how you will do it. This is explained in Chapter 5.

I have discovered, in my work as a therapist, that people need guidance in learning how to communicate with each other on a truly deep, open and honest level. Therefore, I developed a series of questionnaires to help improve your communication skills and awareness.

My extensive experience in the field of "biofeedback," using the mind to control physiological functions, gave me insight into the need to know how to relax and to quiet your mind so your body can enjoy to the full the pleasures of the flesh. I developed relaxation exercises, clearly described and easy to follow, to teach you how to relax your mind and body. To help this relaxation process, I developed exercises which actually train you to become more imaginative and creative, that help you to create images in your mind's eye.

Awareness of my own body and my training in physiology showed me the importance of being able to use the body as effectively as possible, enjoying it to the utmost. I developed a system for the use of the "sex muscles" described, step by step, in Chapter 3.

In addition to working with persons experiencing sexual dysfunctions, impotence, frigidity, etc., I also work with people who have sexual problems which are not considered to be dysfunctions, but which I consider to be problems, because they keep them from enjoying their sexual selves fully.

Such problems include inhibitions, rigidities, repressive attitudes, inability to communicate, inability to ask for what you want, to give as much as you'd like, and to share feelings and desires.

For these situations, I have developed questionnaires to increase communications skills and help you toward greater self-awareness. I also devised the "desensitization" program described in Chapter 20, the chapter on inhibitions.

What began as a series of exercises for persons with certain sexual dysfunctions has evolved into one of the most unusual, systematic approaches to sex therapy today. I have incorporated all of the scientific information you need to know to improve your sexual life. I have developed simple, easy-to-follow exercises and techniques—in a step-by-step approach—to help you reach your own personal goal. I have tested this system and I know it works. Some patients have showed improvement in as short a time as one week. Most take from four to six weeks to complete the program.

There have been some spectacular successes. A nonorgasmic woman came to see me. She had been in traditional analysis for five years, seeing her therapist three times a week. After following the relaxation exercises I developed, she began the masturbation techniques outlined in the chapter on frigidity. She experienced her first orgasm after only one week, following this system.

This woman and the cases described in the chapters dealing with specific dysfunctions such as frigidity are only some of the many people who have benefited from this program. It is a program that works because it has been developed with real people who wanted it to work, who wanted to succeed.

I have made every effort to include every problem presented to me during the testing of the program. Throughout the book, I share with you some of the situations others faced and warn you how to avoid making the same mistakes. I have refined and changed the system so that you won't be faced with many of the problems they faced.

Nothing succeeds like success. Many of my colleagues have incorporated the use of relaxation techniques into their private sex therapy practice and the use of image-making and contracts. Dr. Barbara Hogan has called my technique of "urine control" ingenious, because it is so simple to learn and so effective in the treatment of male dysfunctions such as premature ejaculation and impotence. (You'll read more about this in Chapters 13 and 14.)

This program is for anyone who feels dissatisfied with his or her sex life. It will work for you if you are not seriously disturbed psychologically and if you do not have a physiological dysfunction. If you can commit yourself to the program, if you take yourself seriously enough and follow the instructions and practice the techniques with pleasure, then you can be sure that there is no danger of your being disturbed psychologically. If you have serious problems with commitment, with staying with the program, with helping your partner and working together or with yourself, then I suggest that you seek professional help before continuing with the program.

If you are sexually dysfunctional, this does not mean that you have a physiological problem. If male and you can ejaculate and can attain an erection, then you are not suffering physiologically, although you may be dissatisfied with how you function sexually. If female and you do lubricate upon stimulation and do have sensation in your genital area, then you are probably not physiologically dysfunctional. Further discussion of this is included in the chapters dealing with specific sexual dysfunctions.

Many practicing homosexuals have asked for therapy. Their therapy is exactly the same as for a practicing heterosexual—IF they are coming to therapy to ease a sexual problem or dysfunction. If they are coming to therapy because they no longer want to *be* homosexual, then this help-yourself program is not for them. They must seek more traditional psychotherapy. But a homosexual who is content with his or her sexual preference, but is having performance problems can benefit from this system. Anyone can follow the directions, exercises, techniques and questionnaires regardless of his/her situation: heterosexual, bisexual, with a partner or without a partner.

This book is designed so that you can follow the program, master it, use it to the fullest for your own development, growth and improved sexual life. This program takes you by the hand and leads you, step-by-step, through an entire course of exercises and experiences to a gratifying sex life— the joys and pleasures of satisfying your physical and romantic needs.

This program is not limited to those experiencing a sexual dysfunction or problem. It works for married couples who are bored with each other and take each other for granted. It brings back the zest and excitement they had in their lives when they first met—and more. It works for those who wish their sex life to be better.

You Can Be Your Own Sex Therapist will teach you how to tear down barriers, how to build toward the self-confidence and self-awareness integral to truly enjoying your sensual self.

I would like to say here that you will find throughout this book that I consider everything which is pleasurable and without pain or danger to yourself and others as acceptable and wonderful. But there are certain types of behavior which I consider to be extremely dangerous and which I warn you against—not in terms of being "sick" or "wrong" or "perverse," but in terms of what real pleasure and joy are.

If you are not seriously emotionally disturbed, if you are not physiologically impaired and you truly want to improve your sexual life, this system can work for you too. But there are problems which cannot be solved by help-yourself sex therapy. I indicate what these are throughout the book and want to stress here that, if professional help is indicated, please seek it.

Before getting to work on your own help-yourself therapy program, please read all of Sections I and II, and the chapter in Section III which applies to you, if you are suffering from a specific sexual dysfunction. Then you will be fully aware of the commitment you must make.

When you begin, follow all of the instructions as closely as you possibly can. DO NOT SKIP ANYTHING. DO NOT RUSH ANYTHING. DO NOT IGNORE ANYTHING. Every exercise, every moment that I ask you to spend completing a questionnaire or following an exercise is planned and designed for a specific reason.

The amount of time the program takes to complete is entirely up to you. You may need as little as one week, or as long as six weeks—or more—depending on your problem, how much time you spend on yourself each day and how hard you work. But unless you have a physiological or psychological problem, or an unconscious wish to keep yourself unhappy and unfulfilled, you can succeed—if you follow all of the instructions precisely as they are given. Remember, learn from my experience and from the experience of my clients. *Do not try to develop your own system.* Use this one—it works!

In a clinic or in a sex therapist's private office, this program could cost you as much as $3000. In your own home, you need make no further investment—no equipment, no medication, no medical or psychiatric consultation is required for the majority.

Historically, people have always dealt with their erotic feelings "undercover," so to speak. Most of us are reluctant to share our innermost feelings with strangers, or admit that we want more excitement and pleasure in our sexual lives. This book gives you the opportunity to retain this right to privacy and intimacy. You alone, with your partner, confiding in no one else, can share your love and joy and gain heights of sexual pleasure and freedom.

The benefits of the system are many. The program has worked for hundreds. Its success has been proven. It has given me a great deal of personal satisfaction to see so many people—at such low cost and with such ease—change their lives so dramatically and positively.

This is your system. The program is now yours. Use it well. Use it successfully. Enjoy it. I wish you all the pleasure and success that others have gained.

CHAPTER II

The Physiology of Sex

IN HIS BOOK, *The Function of the Orgasm,* Dr. Wilhelm Reich stated that a person cannot be physically or emotionally healthy unless he experiences frequent and complete orgasms. He defined orgasm as "the capacity for complete discharge of all dammed-up sexual excitation through involuntary pleasurable contractions of the body."

Orgasm, the complete discharge of energy, is necessary for our physical and emotional health, according to Dr. Reich. I agree with him completely, and so do hundreds of other doctors and psychologists. When Dr. Reich wrote *The Function of the Orgasm,* it was a revolutionary book, decades ahead of its time, and did not receive enough attention or acclaim.

Since then, there has been a "sexual revolution." Today all we can learn, all we can do to improve our sexual lives, all we can enjoy is becoming accessible knowledge and a welcome addition to our lives. We are seeking—we are finding.

In this book you will gain a great deal of information about sexual practices. There are techniques for improving and enhancing your sexual life, as well as a systematic program for curing the most common sexual dysfunctions which plague so many. Today, with the new sex therapies, no one need suffer from such a dysfunction.

I'd like to share with you now some of the physiology of sex. I feel strongly that the more you understand the actual reactions of your body to various stimuli, the more you can improve your sexual life. Knowledge of body parts, the most sensitive areas and the reactions which are expected and desired are all awarenesses which can enhance your sexuality.

Let's begin with the genital areas.

12

In the female there are the outer and inner lips along the outside edges of the entrance to the vagina known as the *labia.* The vaginal opening is approximately one inch above the base of these lips. The *urethra,* the opening for urine to pass through, is approximately one inch above the vaginal opening. The *clitoris* is at the head of these lips, almost where the lips come together at the top. The clitoris has a piece of skin over it known as the *clitoral hood.*

This hood is a godsend to women. The clitoris with thousands of nerve endings in its tiny area is exquisitely sensitive. Direct contact with the clitoris might be very painful or, at the least, uncomfortable. This hood allows a woman to be stimulated to the point of excitement while it simultaneously prevents pain.

Another magical touch of mother nature is that all of the nerve endings—or sensory perceptors—in the vagina are located *only* at the mouth of the vagina, within an inch or so of the vaginal entrance. Again, this is to prevent pain. If women had nerve endings throughout the vagina, the pain of childbirth would be much more excruciating. But the way women are created permits the head of the child to pass through the vaginal canal almost entirely before any nerve endings are reached.

This is also one of the reasons why the length of the penis is not at all important to pleasurable sex. Because the nerve endings, the sensitive area, are within an inch or so of the mouth of the vagina, the rest of the vagina receives very little sensation from the inserted penis. Another fact which gives the lie to the mythical benefits of a large penis is the "ballooning" quality of the vagina.

The vagina is shaped like a balloon that has been slightly blown up, one that has air at the end of it. As the penis penetrates, the vagina adapts to accommodate it, as if the balloon were getting fuller at the end. It remains unextended if the penis does not require more room. The walls of the entrance to the vagina stretch only enough to accommodate the penis. Whatever the circumference of the penis, it is not a criterion in the stimulation of the vagina.

The only really essential issue is that you use positions during sexual intercourse which satisfy you best. Since the clitoris needs to be stimulated in order to climax, you should position yourselves so that the clitoris is stimulated as much as possible, and sexual intercourse will be that much more pleasurable. Some positions offer more possibility for this than others. You yourselves must find those positions which are best for you. You can also masturbate or be masturbated during intercourse. Many women and men find this very exciting and satisfying. Experiment until you find the position which is most satisfactory for your own bodies and pleasures.

Speaking of the clitoral orgasm, I feel it is unnecessary to go deeply into the great argument about the vaginal orgasm vs. the clitoral orgasm. As stated above, there is only *one* orgasm and that is achieved through clitoral stimulation. If a woman does have an orgasm during penetration, it is because the thrusts of the penis are pulling down on her labia, which, as they move down, stimulate the clitoris. It is this stimulation which helps to increase the vaginal contractions which are bringing on the orgasm.

During orgasm, the vaginal walls are contracting once every .8 of a second. The contractions of the vagina due to the excitation, increased tension in the muscles and additional blood flow in the genital area are all factors which bring a woman toward a climax.

It is fascinating how perfectly our bodies work. As the female orgasm takes place, the uterus contracts, and thus dips down slightly. As the uterus dips down, the mouth of the cervix dips down too, directly into the vaginal cavity where the semen has been deposited. This movement is a kind of insurance that the sperm will swim through the cervix into the uterus, so that the egg can be fertilized.

Sexual reactions are similar in both the male and the female. Man and woman experience similar sexual stages and feelings.

The penis has several *vesicles* running through it. One carries the blood which causes the erection when blood flow increases as excitation increases. Another is for the urine and the semen. Urine and the semen pass through the same vesicle, though at different times of course. But though the urine and the semen are excreted through the same opening at the tip of the penis and pass through the same vesicle, they originate in different areas of the body.

The vesicle carrying the blood has no outlet. When the erection subsides, the blood returns to the rest of the body through the same vesicle. A similar reaction occurs in the woman. After her climax, the additional blood which has rushed to the genital area returns to the rest of the body.

On the penis, at the very tip, is the *glans*. This is just below the hood and at the very top of the large vein running alongside the penis from base to hood. The glans is very sensitive, since there are many nerve endings in this small area. When the glans is stimulated, the male experiences a great deal of pleasure. This is also the spot to apply pressure to stop ejaculation by using the "thumb treatment" described in Chapter 13, *Premature Ejaculation.*

One of the examinations given to couples who enter sex therapy is an exploratory one. A doctor examines each one of the partners and explains to the other exactly what each part of the body is for and its technical name. An exciting moment in this examination for most of the men is when the doctor allows the male to look into the vagina of the female. It is truly an amazing organ—to think that a child can be delivered from such a small area! The colors of the skin of the cervix, the wonder of what the vagina performs all seem to excite the male in a very romantic and loving way. Men have remarked that they are in awe of what they see, are proud and excited for their women and gain a deep respect for the wonder of the female body.

It is possible for you to do this examination yourselves. Many of the National Organization for Women offices, or women's clinics, or even surgical supply stores, now have available very inexpensive plastic speculums. They are simple instruments to use. Upon insertion of the speculum into the vagina, the walls of the vagina are spread, and it is possible to see into the vaginal cavity up to the mouth of the cervix.

In fact, women are encouraged to do this examination themselves on a weekly basis. When an infection is building up, the mouth of the cervix will actually change in color. This color change is a warning, and if you examine yourself regularly you can treat any infection before it fully develops.

Now, let's look at what happens physiologically when you begin to make love. Thanks to Masters and Johnson and their ingenious research methods, we now know a great deal about our physical processes that was not known before. With the use of films, questionnaires, observations and pictures taken internally, they discovered the following cycles of bodily reactions during lovemaking. These cycles are similar in male and female.

When you first begin to make love, you are beginning what Masters and Johnson call the EXCITEMENT PHASE.

Males: The penis becomes erect as blood begins to fill the vesicle causing the penis to swell. The testicles tend to flatten out and begin to rise. During intense excitement, a very small drop of thick colorless fluid is often emitted from the penis. This comes from the *Cowper's Gland.* It is not a sign of premature ejaculation. It is merely a signal that the body is intensely excited, and is preparing for the seminal emission. Very often, males don't even notice this fluid.

Females: The vaginal walls begin to contract causing a secretion of fluid which lubricates the vagina. The clitoris enlarges and hardens so that it seems to come out further from between the labia. It becomes erect, as the penis does, due to the increased blood flow to the area.

General: The nipples become hardened and erect, breathing quickens, the skin may flush, and you may begin making various sounds.

As you continue lovemaking, you go into what is called the PLATEAU PHASE.

Males: The testes flatten even more and rise up further toward the body. The penis becomes more erect and hardens to its maximum size. Seminal fluid is forming in the vesicle. This is the Premonitory Stage, the point at which the male becomes aware that he needs to stop stimulation or be unable to control ejaculation.

Females: The vaginal cavity is expanding, contractions in the vagina are increasing, lubrication is increased, the labia are swelling and changing color due to additional blood flow in the area. The skin at the entrance to the vagina, where the nerve endings are, is also engorged with blood and deepens in color to dark red.

General: You both have increased heart rate, breathing, higher blood pressure, muscular tension, noises may increase in sound and frequency, a slight rash may be increasing.

You are now at the next stage, the ORGASMIC PHASE.

Males: Blood flow has increased to the point where the body can no longer tolerate any further pressure in the genital area, the seminal vesicles are full, the testes have risen completely up into the body. The semen begins to flow upward, toward the mouth of the seminal vesicle. This is known as "ejaculatory inevitability," since at this point the male cannot control the ejaculation. The penis is contracting once every .8 of a second, the semen begins to spurt out of the tip of the penis and orgasm takes place.

Females: The entire genital area is engorged with blood, the walls of the vagina are contracting once every .8 of a second. The clitoris is enlarged with blood and standing erect, lubrication is greatly increased.

General: The nipples are hardened and erect, a temporary skin rash may occur, itching may occur, so may very heavy breathing, loud sounds, increased heartbeat, raised blood pressure. The anus contracts, the mouth and eyes may open and close involuntarily in response to pleasurable feelings. Coloration of the skin and the itching are due to the rush of blood flowing from the genital area to the rest of the body.

When the genital area cannot tolerate any increased blood flow, when muscular tension is at its peak of endurance, the body lets go, and the blood returns to the rest of the body. This instant release—the spasm of letting go, the total relaxation of all muscles, all tensions, all pain—is the orgasm.

You may feel all of these reactions, or a few of them. You may feel additional reactions. However, if you do not experience the spasm of the body, the instant release of tension, then you are probably not experiencing orgasm. Orgasm is the result of the rush of blood from the genital area and the release of muscular tension. As the muscles relax, as the blood makes its flight back toward the rest of the body, YOU take a flight to ecstasy. This is the orgasm. As you lie in this state of

pleasure and joy, fully sensing the magnificence of the pre-
ceding moments, you are in what is called THE RESOLU-
TION PHASE.

At this point, everything that was happening up until now
reverses. The genital areas which were engorged with blood
now lose this blood and skin-color returns to normal; the
testicles come down and become looser and enlarged; the
penis returns to half its normal erect size immediately and to
its normal size within a half hour; the heart rate begins slow-
ing down, blood pressure decreases. You are in a quiet state of
pleasure.

Few men can return to the excitation stage or the orgasmic
stage immediately after orgasm. This is known as being "multiply orgasmic," having one orgasm after the other without
any time lapse between. Multiple orgasms are possible for
women, though, because women do not have to go through
each of the four stages described here, nor do they require a
"refractory stage."

In order for a man to reach orgasm, he must go through all
four stages, and he must also experience a refractory—
resting—stage after each orgasm. Males require varied
amounts of time to rest in this refractory stage. During this
phase, the body relaxes and regenerates itself. For younger
men, the time required is very short; older men generally
require a longer rest period. Often when the time of the
refractory phase increases, men worry, wondering if something is wrong. Please be assured that this strictly physiological
function is very necessary and normal. The male body
needs time before it can be aroused again. Enjoy the time of
quiet and peacefulness your body is experiencing after
orgasm.

To clarify your understanding of your physiological responses let me emphasize certain facts. Too often we speak of
the penis and the female *genitalia.* This is wrong. The female
genital organ comparable to the penis is the clitoris—not the
vagina or anything else. More specifically, it is comparable to
the most sensitive area of the penis—the glans—so perhaps we
should speak of the glans and the clitoris.

The vagina best compares to the scrotal sac; here, as in the
male scrotal sac, fluid is produced. Orgasm for both men and

women is the same: as blood rushes back to the rest of the body from the genital areas, the body reacts by "jumping," going into spasms.

Excitation is similar for both sexes too. In men, the penis becomes erect, women become lubricated. Both can experience all of the other physical reactions described. In fact, women have an erection of sorts since the clitoris does enlarge and rise up from its resting place. Similarly, for men, the glans on the penis becomes enlarged and more and more sensitive to the touch.

Please don't begin comparing your physiological responses to those described here! Don't watch for the signals discussed above. If you have not experienced the intense feeling of orgasm, the following chapters will help you to reach this peak of pleasure. But don't worry or analyze your every breath as you are making love: "Am I breathing fast enough?" or "Are her nipples hard enough?" or "Has my anus contracted this time or not?"

These are the kinds of questions I've been told some people are concerned about during loving. Please don't allow this to happen. Never mind what your physiological responses are. Be loving, be giving, be accepting of all pleasure during lovemaking. Don't worry about the physiology of sex. Be aware of your body, the various stages of sex, and the wonder of your body which makes it all possible. This awareness can aid you toward better loving. But don't compare your reactions to what you have read or heard about. Don't worry about various stimuli, or physical responses, that may not be present. Allow yourself to *be*. Use this program and watch your pleasure increase daily.

Your pleasures and the way in which you have them are your own. You *own* them. They are not for anyone else, or to be experienced as anyone else does. Loving is personal, experiencing is personal, your own physiological responses are personal. If you want changes, you'll make them by following this program, but don't judge yourself or fault yourself for seeking change. What is happening now is one factor, and what will be happening in the future is another. You can change whatever you want to change, or maintain what you want to maintain.

You Can Be Your Own Sex Therapist sets out a program which can help you to see what you would like to be different in your sexual and sensual life and what you would like to retain. Your goals are within your reach with the use of the book you now hold in your hands. Be your own sex therapist. You can, you know!

CHAPTER THREE

Put Power in Your "Sex" Muscles

AN anonymous writer recently put it this way: "What! Fat, forty-three and I dare to think I'm still a person?"

To this I shout a resounding, "Yes!" Everyone alive—everyone—is entitled to all of the rights and feelings and pleasures available to him.

No matter what your age or the condition of your body, you will derive maximum pleasure from sex and feel more like a person, after you have learned to control your "sex" muscles. This control is an adjunct to the other pleasures and joys you will glean from the techniques and procedures described in this book. All of these pleasures are for you. You are entitled to them. You deserve them. You can have them.

In the female, the "sex" muscle is the *pubococcygeous* and in the male it is the *bulbocavernosus.* These muscles control the walls of the vagina and the penis respectively. The greater the control you have of them, the more enjoyment you will have, and the more pleasure you can give your partner. Control of these muscles allows you to be a more sexually expressive person. You will have a talent which is simple to develop and wonderfully useful and exciting.

You can be a gifted lover to your partner and a more sensual person for yourself. Control of these muscles will not only help you to enjoy sex more, but can also help you to want sex more. We all know the feeling of being "too tired," or "too nervous," or "too angry" for sex. We also know that there is no release like the joy and pleasure of good sex. But certain emotional situations are difficult to control, and we turn

21

ourselves off to the thrill of good sex. If you allow your body to work for you, your mind can let go of whatever the emotion is that keeps you from wanting sex at the moment.

Men and women can use these sex muscles to excite themselves, so that the body will want sex and whatever the mind is disturbed about will not seem so important. When females contract their sex muscle, they cause the walls of the vagina to contract which, in turn, causes an excretion of fluid. This is exactly what happens to the vagina during the excitement stage of sex.

Exercising the sex muscle is equally as effective for men, I have found. As males pull on this muscle, they begin to experience an erection, become excited and want to enjoy the pleasures of lovemaking.

Self-excitation is a very important use of control of the sex muscle. For example, it can stimulate desire in couples who have been together so long they have lost the excitement or the desire for sex. But self-excitation is only one use. Control of the sex muscles is important in the cure of several dysfunctions: premature ejaculation and impotence in men and frigidity in women.

Control of these muscles is gained very easily. Actually both men and women use these muscles a great deal of the time although they are not aware that they are using them. One of the most frequent uses of these muscles is in controlling the flow of urine. This happens to you whenever you feel you have to urinate but can't because of time or place. You "hold it in." You are holding it in with your sex muscle.

Try the following exercises to experience the sensation of controlling these muscles. I developed these myself as a unique and simple method to teach you control:

(1.) Go to the bathroom when you don't feel the need to void. Allow a small amount of urine to pass and then pull back. Don't allow any more urine to pass. Again, allow a small amount of urine to pass and pull back. Continue this until you have voided completely.

Every time you pull back, you are using your sex muscles. You will find that this is simple to master. You will become aware of what it feels like as you pull back. It is important that you become familiar with the feeling. You should feel a tightening inside the vagina if you're a woman, tightening behind your testicles, just in front of the anus, if you're a man.

(2.) Now that you are familiar with the feeling you experience when you use this muscle, try to use it as much as possible. As you sit, merely try to pull on the muscle the same way you pulled when you stopped the flow of urine.

Females: Pretend you are pushing the walls of your vagina together, as in an isometric exercise. Tighten your thighs as though pushing them downward on the chair. Pretend you are pulling your pubic area upwards.

Males: Pretend you are pushing your testicles together, or pulling upwards on your penis.

You should be able to sense the feelings as your sex muscle tightens. I have not met anyone who has been unable to follow these directions and experience the sensations of tightening and pulling as described. If you are having trouble, please continue these techniques until you begin to experience the sensation. You will be able to if you continue the exercises.

(For more about the control of these muscles, please see the chapter on premature ejaculation and on impotence in males, and the chapter on frigidity in females.)

Once you have mastered control of these muscles in the ways described, the next step is to gain control of them during intercourse. This is much more difficult. Once the penis penetrates the vagina, it is more difficult to contract the vaginal walls—and more difficult to move the penis during penetration. Therefore, you should have gained muscle control before doing this during penetration.

Females can practice this in a gradual way, following a much simpler set of exercises that will gradually build up the control of the sex muscles during intercourse:

(1.) Begin by inserting a small object such as a small plastic cylinder, a cocktail stirrer (sterilized of course), or a tampon into the mouth of the vagina—just an inch or two.

(2.) Now, pull on this muscle as you did when there was nothing penetrating. Continue doing this until you feel you have gained control sufficiently to truly experience the contractions, tightening and loosening as you did when you were using the muscle for controlling urine flow, etc.

(3.) Now insert a larger object. Perhaps if you started with a cocktail stirrer, you will now go to a tampon, or to a larger size tampon, or the cardboard covering the tampon. Use your own judgment, constantly increasing the size of the object and increasing your control of this muscle.

(4.) If you would like to test your own control, insert your fingers into your vagina. Use one finger at first, then insert two fingers. Now test the control you have gained of this muscle. Can you feel the walls of your vagina tightening against your fingers?

Remember, as with any muscle development program, you should continue to use this muscle daily. You can pull on this muscle whenever you think about it, regardless of where you are or who you are with. You can "pull" and feel the sensation of what controlling this muscle can do for you. Practice gives more and more control. You can increase control of this muscle as much as you like.

For males, follow the procedure as often as possible of pulling on this muscle. Flex the muscle as you would your arm muscle. The more often you flex it or use it, the stronger it will become. You can increase control to the point of being able to move your penis back and forth toward your body and away from your body. With even greater practice you can learn to move your penis from side to side as well.

Can you imagine your partner's pleasure, as well as your own, if you can learn to control your penis while penetrating and thrusting? This can be done, but as in the case of females, it is much more difficult to control your movements while penetrating. Therefore, it is important to exercise this muscle as often as possible and to develop control as completely as possible.

Women derive a great deal of pleasure from the penis as it moves around inside the vagina. A man can maintain an erection much longer when he can control this muscle and derive pleasure from such control, as well as from the various movements he can effect. Again, it is most essential in the control and cure of various dysfunctions.

I have discussed the joys of sex, the fact that you deserve pleasures of the flesh, and various exercises which can aid you to build up your physiological tools for orgasm. In the following chapters, you'll strengthen your mental and physical facilities for the joyful sex life which is your birthright. Don't deprive yourself of it. Please remember to use whatever birth control method you prefer, if any. Also, please be aware of the high incidence of venereal disease if you are involved with more than one sexual partner. Use all that you have and all that you will read here. The program is yours. Profit as fully as possible from it. And now you begin. . . .

Section II

THE PROGRAM

CHAPTER FOUR

And Now You Begin

SEX is a very personal and individual experience. Only you can know what it means to you, what you want from it and what you are willing to give to it. *You Can Be Your Own Sex Therapist* is designed to help you to help yourself toward a fuller, more exciting, more satisfying sexual and sensual life. It is a simplified, step-by-step series of exercises which I have designed to be used easily and successfully.

But your sex life, your sexual needs, your sexual fantasies, hopes and dreams are completely yours. Only you can know them. Therefore, only you can best fulfill these hopes and dreams.

At this point, YOU begin. You begin to take responsibility for yourself and say that you and only you can now follow through in this "Help Yourself Sex Therapy." I have devised a system which I know is successful. But you must use it properly. You are on your own.

The first step is to complete the following questionnaire. It explores every aspect of your sexual goals and mental attitudes. It is designed deliberately to delve deeply into your inner self, to trigger off memories, feelings and thoughts which you didn't realize you had. It is demanding, but can lead to valuable insights. It is relentless in its attempt to find out all that you can discover about your sexual goals.

This questionnaire helps you to focus on yourself and what you really want and need. It will help you to crystallize your thoughts about sex and your goals in this program.

The questions are difficult. The answers may not be readily accessible to you—you may have to probe for them. The knowledge you gain from completing this questionnaire may

29

even be painful to you. All of this is necessary, however, for you to have the complete success you want. Learn as much as you can about yourself. Do not skip questions, or respond with a glib, quick answer.

Please take your time with this questionnaire. Be serious about it. Respond to each question several times, if you are not satisfied with your original response. If you cannot answer immediately, give yourself time to think about it. Be sure that each answer is as complete, as honest, as direct as it is possible for you to give.

If you feel that any of the answers are too personal, too private for you to share with anyone, keep these responses to yourself. Don't share them even with your partner. But—and this is very important—be sure to answer each question for yourself. The more you learn about yourself, the easier it will be for you to complete this program with success and joy.

If you feel embarrassed about any of your responses, if you become aware of inhibitions or feelings of shame which you did not realize you had, please read Chapters 19 and 20, dealing with fetishes and inhibitions.

If, when answering these questions, you don't learn a great deal about yourself, can't focus on what your problems are or what you want from sex therapy, then please complete the questionnaire again at another time. Compare your answers the second time to your answers the first time. Complete the questionnaire a third time, if you feel you can learn still more about yourself, and again compare the answers. You will be amazed at what you will learn each and every time you complete this questionnaire.

If you still have trouble completing the questionnaire, please go on to the next chapter, and make a contract with yourself that you "will really try."

The "Let's Really Try" Contract Number II is described in Chapter 5. You may need this commitment to yourself to encourage you to work seriously toward your goal.

Read each of the questions completely before answering. Think about your response. Take yourself seriously and be aware that you are now taking the first step in "Help Yourself Sex Therapy." Step with a sure stride. Good luck!

(1.) Is sex what you want it to be for you?

(2.) If not, what changes do you want to make in your sex life?

(3.) What type of foreplay do you engage in?

(4.) Do you want any changes in these activities?

(5.) Is the foreplay long enough for you?

(6.) How can you increase the foreplay if you'd like to?

(7.) What activities would you like to add to your foreplay?

(8.) What embarrasses you?

(9.) What part of your body are you ashamed of?

(10.) What part of your body do you like the most?

(11.) I would never want anyone to see my————.

(12.) What about that part of your body? What's wrong with it?

(13.) What is your expectation of what would happen if someone looked at this part?

(14.) During foreplay I wish that I could————.

(15.) During intercourse I wish that I could————.

(16.) I do/don't like to masturbate during sex with a partner.

(17.) I know I have problems because————.

(18.) I don't have a problem, but I'd like to improve ————.

(19.) I'm inhibited about the following sexual activities: ————.

(20.) When my partner————I get embarrassed.

(21.) I like the following positions:————.

(22.) I would like to try the following positions:————.

(23.) I don't believe the following about sex:————.

(24.) Are love and sex the same to you?

(25.) Are you relaxed during sex?

(26.) What are you thinking about during sex?

(27.) Do you have sexual fantasies?

(28.) I am reading this book because————.

(29.) I hope that when I am finished with this book I will— ————.

(30.) I am willing to give the following amount of time to Do-It-Yourself Sex Therapy:————.

(31.) I want my partner to————.

(32.) I'm afraid that————.

(33.) I have the following questions to ask————.

(34.) I think I have a dysfunction because————.

(35.) I am influenced by what I read, what I hear and what I see. Because of this I————.

(36.) I hope that my sex life————.

(37.) Do you masturbate? Do you like it?

(38.) Does your partner know you masturbate? Why/Why not?

(39.) How do you feel about pleasuring? Being pleasured?

(40.) Do you like sex?

(41.) Do you deserve to enjoy the pleasures of the flesh?

(42.) Do you masturbate during sex?

(43.) Would you like to masturbate in front of your partner?

(44.) Would you like your partner to masturbate in front of you?

(45.) Do you have any fantasies you wish your partner would fulfill for you?

(46.) What is your most frequent fantasy?

(47.) What do you like to do after sex?

(48.) Are you satisfied with what your partner does when it's over?

(49.) Write a sentence now explaining what you want after sex.

(50.) If your partner says "no" to sex, does that mean you are not loved?

(51.) Do you feel spiteful or want to retaliate if your partner says no?

(52.) Are *you* being rejected if your sexual advances are rejected?

(53.) Do you feel that you're a "sick" person?

(54.) What makes you sick?

Males:

(55.) Can you get an erection?

(56.) Can you have an ejaculation?

Females:

(57.) Do you lubricate inside your vagina?

(58.) Do you feel any pleasure at all when you touch your clitoris?

(If the answer to any of the above paired male/female questions is "No," then you may have a physical impairment and should definitely consult a medical doctor before continuing in "Help Yourself Sex Therapy." However, if the answer is yes, despite other problems you may have— premature ejaculation, impotence, frigidity, or nonorgasmic symptoms—then you are probably not physically impaired and this system can be of help to you too.)

To give you an idea of how much you can begin to learn about your personality by replying to these questions, here are sample answers to two of the questions which may seem difficult to answer at first glance.

Question: "I am influenced by what I read, what I hear, and what I see. Because of this——."

Answer: "I am influenced by what I read, by what others tell me, by everything. I don't really feel for myself or think for myself sometimes, and I think this stands in my way of enjoying sex. I am making love and thinking: 'Am I doing this right? Is she really liking it? Should I change what I'm doing?' etc. I don't really trust myself, because I'm so busy comparing myself to all of the stories I hear about sex, and probably most of them are all lies anyhow. So, because of this, I feel that I miss out a lot on the real sensations of the moment, which I can't be experiencing because I'm so busy thinking."

(This problem is discussed further in the chapter on inhibitions.)

This man learned to relax, to clear his mind, and be with the sensations of his body using this program.

Another question which may be difficult for you to understand is: "How do you feel about pleasuring? Being pleasured?"

Sample reply: "I find it pretty easy to give pleasure, but when someone wants to "pleasure" me, to give me pleasure, I get embarrassed and I begin to squirm and can't take it for very long. I usually stop them by saying 'That's enough thanks' or something like that."

The concept of pleasuring and being pleasured is very exciting and rewarding. Giving to another and getting from another are wonders of our life and some of the true joys of living. Without sharing, what do we really have? Please think seriously about this question. Is it easy for you to receive? Can you say "Thank you" without being embarrassed? Can you give without *expecting* to get back? Can you "pleasure and be pleasured"?

If you find it difficult, you can use the desensitizing approach in Chapter 19. Build up your ability to give and to get slowly and gradually, following the process described.

Again this questionnaire is imperative. Your responses must be as complete and as honest as possible. You must know what your sexual life is all about *before* you proceed to the remainder of this book.

Say you have completed the questionnaire as fully as you possibly can. You've answered each question honestly, delved into your deepest self to discover new things about yourself, and now you have your answers. Now what?

First—and most important—you know what's right about your sex life. You have discovered what you like, what you enjoy, what is good at this moment. Then you have described what is wrong about your sex life. You know what you don't like, what changes you would like to make, and what activities and pleasures you would like to add. You also know what may be impeding your full enjoyment of sex.

Finally, you have uncovered any inhibitions you may have, any embarrassments you suffer from any restrictions you have put on your sex life. If you are not clear about any of these points, answer the questions again.

Now, please read the rest of this book. Do not engage in any of the activities. Do not practice any of the techniques. Merely read through the entire text. As you read, you will realize how the techniques and concepts can help you. For example, you will read about various ways to increase communication. These will help you to share with your partner your new awareness of the sexual activities you would like to engage in and the changes you would like to make in your sexual life.

Incidentally, if your partner does not wish to be involved in this program, you can work alone for new sexual vigor. Eventually, your newly-developed skills will add much joy to your sexual relationship.

As you read through this book, you will discover the systems I have developed for desensitizing yourself to various inhibitions, fears, embarrassments, or restrictions which you may have. You will be able to apply these systems to the information you have learned about yourself by completing the questionnaire. There may be a particular part of your body which embarrasses you. You can desensitize yourself to this. There may be a sexual activity which you have felt inhibited about indulging in. You can desensitize yourself to this, if you wish to.

You will discover how to relax and feel comfortable so that you can enjoy sex fully and increase and enhance your sensual pleasure. You can focus on those sensual activities which you desire, as indicated by the responses on your questionnaire.

If you have a sexual dysfunction, such as premature ejaculation or frigidity, you will find in this book the system I have developed which can help you to help yourself toward a complete cure.

As you read, be aware of how you can apply what you read to yourself. This is *your* sex therapy. You are your own therapist. You *must* probe your inner self as a therapist would. You *must* become as aware as possible of yourself, so that you can direct yourself to the techniques and systems in this book most appropriate to your needs. You must use the information I have developed to the fullest. Remember, you are responsible for yourself, so be good to yourself.

CHAPTER FIVE

The Making of Contracts in Sex Therapy

A student in college begins his term paper the night before it is due. The secretary chats on the phone for an hour, then rushes through the ten letters she must finish before 5 P.M. The businessman calls for a plane reservation the day before he has to leave.

Some of these people are lucky. Some students do manage to stay up all night and finish their papers—and even do a good job. Some secretaries can rush through their work and get it done properly. Sometimes airlines do have reservations a few hours before they are needed. But most often life does not work this way.

Without planning, without allowing for enough time and materials, without anticipation of pressure and the possibility of failure, very little can be achieved. It is a very rare success that just "comes to you." The majority of people who get what they want, accomplish what they want and feel proud and joyful with their success, are people who plan and work and plan some more. There are few miracles.

Successful sex, a joyful and pleasurable sexual life, is a good example of this. People who work for a good and exciting and successful sex life have a much greater chance of it than those who ignore their sexual selves.

Of course there are people who cannot benefit from this help yourself plan. They have serious physical malfunctions, or deep psychological problems, or are not truly interested and concerned enough about their own physical pleasure to work at it. There may be other hindrances to the successful completion of this program which I have not encountered in my practice.

But my experience with hundreds of patients has been that if you take yourself seriously, follow the program as it is planned for you, want to succeed, and are not suffering from any serious psychological or physical problems, you will benefit greatly from this program. Colleagues with whom I have discussed it, and shared many of the ideas with, have agreed that it is an effective program. Dr. Alex Comfort, the editor of *Joy of Sex*, states that the new sex therapy techniques lend themselves to a do-it-yourself approach. I have taken these techniques, added my own, structured and simplified them into an easy to follow program, learning from my patients' successes and failures.

You will discover that these sex therapy techniques can help you enjoy your life more completely and joyfully as have so many others: married and unmarried, with children and without children, young and old, male and female.

All benefited from this systematic approach to sex therapy. All of them followed the first and basic premise on which it is founded: there must be a very high level of cooperation, caring and concern for each other and for yourself, so that you will be able to react for and with each other as prescribed.

To put this basic premise into action and to help you discover exactly how it can work, you will want to consider the formation of contractual agreements between you and your partner. With the contracts, you can plan what work you are going to do together, agree how you are going to do it, decide on what you are willing to give, and how you are willing and able to help each other.

Words such as "help each other" and "communicate" with your partner are used frequently throughout this book. But if you are working alone, if you do not have a permanent sexual partner, most of these exercises and techniques can apply to you too. I have worked with almost two hundred patients who did not have permanent partners, using the help yourself techniques, and they all benefited from them. So, please, follow as many of the techniques as you can, complete the questionnaires, do the exercises, following the program as fully as possible.

Although you may not be communicating your answers to someone else, you will discover so much about yourself that your communication skills will increase in your social and work situations. You will also find that this self-knowledge, this self-awareness will help your confidence.

The contracts discussed in this chapter can be executed by someone alone. Even without a partner, a written contract helps you to focus, provides a time limit, and helps you to make a commitment to yourself, which is essential. So, if you do not have a permanent partner, do not neglect any part of Contracts I and II. They are necessary for all.

In addition to the following contracts, if you are female and are having problems with attaining orgasm, or feel that you are frigid, please turn to Chapter 16 and complete the questionnaire when you are ready to begin your program.

These contracts are *absolutely* necessary. The commitment which you make as you form the contract is the foundation on which you and your partner will stand during "Help Yourself Sex Therapy." This commitment to yourself and to each other must be clear and precise. It must be very personal and individualized to your own needs. It must define how you are willing to proceed with each other and how you are willing to fulfill each other's needs.

You must decide about all of these factors as you go from one level to the next in this program.

You must be responsible and honor the agreements you make with your partner as you do those with yourself. You must be willing to put forth the effort to make the contract rewarding and meaningful to both of you. Simple, precise procedures for drawing up these contracts are outlined in this chapter. Examples of such contracts are included. It is, however, your responsibility to follow and fulfill your contractual commitment.

CONTRACT I:
THE NON-DEMAND, NON-SEXUAL CONTRACT

At the beginning of "Help Yourself Sex Therapy," it is very important that the partner who is experiencing the need for sexual improvement not feel any pressure or sense of failure about it. Therefore, all sexual activity should be avoided by the partners.

This agreement is of the utmost importance. If the dysfunctioning partner knows that for a week or two, he/she will not be pressured to "perform," will not be faced with any further failure, that he/she will be free to enjoy the pleasures of loving and giving in sensual ways, he/she will then—and only then—be able to break down the walls which are keeping him/her from fulfillment.

The purpose of the *Non-Demand, Non-Sexual Contract* is to provide an environment in which both of you may be able to break the "vicious circle" which can sometimes disrupt a couple's sexual relationship. What frequently happens is that one partner will—usually unknowingly—put pressure on the other partner to "perform" better, which, in turn, causes the other to withdraw. This withdrawal in its turn causes the original partner to have a greater need for sexual improvement—which then puts more pressure on the other partner.

Whatever started the "vicious circle" should not be important to you—or even to a sex therapist. The only concern should be to relieve the unhappy partner of pressure to perform. The pressure stays off until all of the exercises for Contracts I and II are successfully completed.

Persons who are not dysfunctional and who have satisfactory sex lives can gain from these contracts. How? They find that by abstaining from sexual activity for awhile, they can develop their sensuality to a more intense and pleasurable pitch. We make contacts through our senses. There is no other way. The more tuned in we are to our senses—our sensuality—the more pleasurable our lives become and the more satisfactory our relationships. As you follow these exercises, your awareness levels will rise to heights you never dreamed possible. The non-sexual aspect of this gives you a new perspective on life and helps toward the heightened development of sensuality and pleasure.

Here is an example of a *Non-Demand, Non-Sexual Contract:*

"We mutually agree that there will be no sexual activity whatsoever until we have completed all of the procedures prescribed up to and including Contract Number II. Neither one of us will seek sexual climax in any way, nor will either of us masturbate unless it is *without* the other's knowledge."

I learned from experience that if a couple is working on a given situation, and the partner free of the sexual inability begins to masturbate, the dysfunctional partner feels guilty, threatened, and more pressured.

Discuss the contract you draw up with each other. There will be questions you will want to ask each other:

(1.) Will you feel deprived if we don't have any sex at all?

(2.) Will you be angry with me?

(3.) How can I help to deal with the anger, if any?

(4.) Do you really want to help yourself by helping me?

(5.) Can you give something in exchange for sex?

(6.) If you want something else, what is it?

(7.) Do you want to set a time limit for the contract? (No less than a week minimum, no more than two weeks for most people.)

(8.) What if we haven't achieved success in that amount of time?

(9.) When will we be able to work at these procedures?

(10.) Do you feel it will benefit both of us, or just me?

These are some of the questions I have been presented with by couples, but you can be assured that this contract is most easily agreed upon by sharing your feelings and responding honestly to these and any other questions you may have. As soon as you know what you expect and want from each other and take responsibility for what is required of you, you are well on the way to successful "Help Yourself Sex Therapy."

This contract can enrich any relationship because you are sharing and communicating in new ways and making commitments to each other to grow and change together.

Sexual improvement is not "his" or "her" responsibility but YOURS! If one of you is not able to enjoy sex to the fullest, the other will probably not be able to either. Consequently, in addition to the *Non-Demand, Non-Sexual Contract,* you will want to agree to put forth an honest effort toward making

"Help Yourself Sex Therapy" work. That agreement is the object of *Contract Number II, "Let's Really Try."*

CONTRACT NUMBER II:
THE "LET'S REALLY TRY" CONTRACT

This contract is written right after Contract Number I, the *Non-Demand, Non-Sexual Contract.* Both are in force simultaneously. Writing this contract can be an important experience. If you are working alone, it will be valuable because you will learn so much about yourself and your preferences. If you are working with a partner, you will communicate with each other in a way that will help you to better understand each other's needs and desires. To write this contract, you must come to terms with each other—and yourself—on several very important points:

(1.) *When you will work with the techniques of sex therapy.* Do not treat this casually. You must make a firm commitment to set aside a certain part of every day for yourself for the specific purpose of following the sex therapy procedures.

(2.) *How you will follow the procedures.*
What this means essentially is:

A. Will you read the various instructions, the relaxation techniques and the questions to each other?

B. Will you tape them and listen to them, doing the exercises together? (See Chapter 6 for specific instruction on taping the exercises for your own use.)

C. Will you follow the recommendation that you have a tape recorder available to record your conversations and responses?

(3.) *What system of compromise will you use?*
There will be many times when compromise will be necessary. For example: One of you may wish to experience the Sensual Exercises for longer periods of time than the other. One of you may wish to bathe while the other will prefer showers. One of you may wish to be massaged with oil while the other dislikes the feel of oil.

These things must all be considered as you discuss the

various techniques and procedures. If you agree beforehand that you will compromise with each other, share experiences and the advised activities, you will avoid many problems which might otherwise arise.

Many couples agree to do everything, regardless of predisposed feelings, and stop if they truly cannot continue. Others agree to "swap": if he does something that she wants, then she does something that he wants. Others prefer to try to experience the situations without judgment, feeling that they are embarking on a new adventure. They find compromise is often not necessary with this attitude. Find your own system of working with each other, thereby guaranteeing your success together.

The terms of Contract II should state explicitly the time that you will set aside to follow the necessary procedures, a firm commitment that nothing short of a serious emergency will preclude the time agreed upon. The contract is a firm commitment to each other, so that both of you will benefit as fully as possible from your sex therapy.

For example, your contract may specify the following:

"We agree that at 11 P.M. every evening we will begin relaxation techniques."

"We agree that we will awaken one hour early every morning so that we can follow the procedures in Chapters 6 to 8."

"We agree to spend every Saturday morning (when the children are at their grandmother's) following the procedures."

"We agree to play together every evening from 9 to 11 P.M."

These are samples from actual contracts. Notice that they vary according to specific needs and availability of time. One couple could not find time together except on Saturday morning, so they didn't try to commit themselves to more than that. They did manage to follow certain exercises more often, but the initial contract was made so that they would not feel pressured.

Do not make a contract for time spent with these procedures that is not realistic or which will make you feel pressured. This is very important. You alone can judge and must decide realistically when you can be alone, where and for how long.

Item Number 2, "How you will follow the procedures," may

be dealt with in a variety of ways. For example, you may include the following in this section of your *"Let's Really Try"* Contract:

"We'll do everything exactly as the book tells us to do it."

"We'll record the exercises on tapes and listen to them together."

"We'll read to each other during those portions of the program requiring specific techniques."

"We will try all of the procedures but if anything seems distasteful or wasteful, we will stop it, if one of us wants to."

(This was written by one couple who both felt they wanted "escape" clauses in the program. Again, I stress, you must respect each other and your individual needs and preferences. But I also stress that if you are working together in the true spirit of giving and taking, you will sincerely try, and not just perfunctorily go through something and quickly decide it's not for you.)

In answer to Item Number 3, "What system of compromise will you use?" typical responses are:

"We will give in to each other if one of us really feels it is important."

"We will fully discuss the situation and make our decision as each situation comes up, keeping in mind that this is for *us,* and we both want to succeed."

This is, of course, the most difficult section of the contract.

Remember that there are essential ingredients in this program and that success depends on the amount of the ingredients you put into it. The system is here, described step-by-step. Your responsibility is to care a great deal for yourself, to want to have a more enjoyable and fulfilling life and to care a great deal for your partner, so that you will both benefit and develop your potential to the fullest.

Write Contract II for yourselves, in your own words, fitting your needs. Remember, if you are working alone, the contract is still necessary. You must make a commitment to yourself to work at a specified time and for a specified time each day. Essentially, what you are agreeing to in Contract II is to respect and care for each other in a tender and giving experience of sensuality and love.

While working on Contracts I and II, you will be experiencing all of the procedures covered in Chapters 6, 7, and 8. You will be doing sensate focus exercises, completing questionnaires, developing the art of image-making and creativity, and living together in a close and communicative environment which will enhance all of your moments together.

This section of the program can take as little as one week to complete; two is average for most people. It is truly an individual experience. Do not go on to Contract III in Chapter 11 until you have mastered all of the procedures in Chapters 6, 7, 8, and 9.

Be patient with yourself. Learn to enjoy the pleasures of slow and easy breathing, to experience your fantasy life fully, to be bathed in oil, or massaged with powder. Relax and learn to enjoy the scents and sounds and views of your world. Slowly and intensely experience your own body, as well as your partner's. The following chapters are yours for pleasure and joy. Make the most of them.

CHAPTER 6

Intensify Your Sensuality and Sexuality

YOUR enjoyment of making love—and of sex—is largely dependent on the sensations you experience. Sensations may be increased or decreased according to your level of awareness of your feelings—and according to your ability to intensify this awareness. It is with your senses that you make all contact. The keener your senses are, the more intense and enjoyable any contact will be.

For example, stop now and smell the air around you. Were you aware of any odors before following this direction? Stop again and feel the texture of this book. Feel the page you are reading, feel the spine of the book, feel the inside of the cover, feel the outside of the cover. Were you aware of the multiplicity of tactile sensations available to you just by touching the various parts of this book?

Try another experiment. Let your tongue roam around inside your mouth. Feel the hardness of your teeth, the rough bumpy feeling of your palate, the smoothness of your teeth, the feeling of wetness or dryness in your mouth, the dents and grooves along your teeth. Let your teeth scrape along the top of your tongue. Were you aware of the many sensations you could experience merely by exploring your own mouth?

Now concentrate on the base of your spine. See whether the position you are sitting in is comfortable. (If you just moved to a more comfortable position, smile.)

All of the things you just "experienced or felt" have been "happening" to you since you began reading this chapter— long before that in the case of "experiencing" your mouth.

In essence, your mind and body are constantly being stimulated by a number of verbal, visual, tactile (touch) and olfactory (smell) sensations. Your body, however, tends to focus on and "feel" only a few of the large number of stimulants to which it is exposed. In psychology, the process of recognizing the experience of only a few stimulants is called "selective perception."

The purpose of this chapter is to help you to learn how to control your selective perception habits so you may increase your awareness of potentially very sensual activities. For whatever reasons, you have probably learned not to experience many exciting sensations. Quite simply you can change this "dull" habit by increasing awareness of your sensations, by developing your knowledge of techniques which intensify sensations and by increasing your interest in sensuality. You can learn to "sense" yourself in a much fuller and more pleasurable way and to "sense" your partner more fully, thereby increasing your pleasure.

If you are aware of the taste in your mouth, the touch on your skin, or the scent in the air, your senses are being utilized fully. Your sensual self is operating and your enjoyment of the sensual pleasures of your life is great. Too few of us, though, are truly aware of the senses through which we make all contact with the world. We underutilize the marvelous tools they are.

Being sensual is being aware—fully aware—of all of the sensations around us and within us. Being sensual is being delighted and thrilled and excited with the pleasures our bodies contact daily. The pleasures of sight and sound, smell, touch, and taste are all within our reach each moment, yet we ignore them and do not receive what they offer. Sensual people are aware, in contact with the environment and with their own bodies. A sensual person uses all of the "sense abilities" available to him.

Sexuality is similar. A sexual person also uses all of the sense abilities available to him but on a rather different level. The sexual person must be sensual first before he can be sexual. If you are unable to make contact with your world through your senses, it is very difficult to be aware of your levels of sexual excitation and sexual pleasures. You must be aware of the

sensations which pleasure you—the ones which turn you on—
to enjoy the full pleasures of the flesh.

Sexuality is in essence, to me, a combination of your sensual
self and your physical or erotic self. It is the ability to feel your
body and to be able to control its responses as you like to attain
the greatest joy and pleasure.

This is accomplished by developing your sensuality, by
becoming aware of your body and your physical responses.

Memorize this sentence and make it a part of your life: "I
will remember to pleasure myself as much as possible by truly
sensing during my waking hours."

It may sound impossible to you, but it's not. Think about it
in practical terms. The next time you sit down to eat a meal,
say to yourself: "I will pleasure myself as much as possible, by
truly tasting this food." If you remember to say this before
each meal, you will begin to be aware of how much tasting you
had been missing. You will realize that a great deal of the food
you eat is merely chewed and swallowed. How often do you let
the food roll around in your mouth, savoring the juices and
the flavor, allowing the taste of it to penetrate your taste buds
and be enjoyed to the fullest? Most people do not remember
to pleasure themselves fully during meals.

In the same way, many people drive along the same roads
day after day and are unaware of the magnificent architecture
of the buildings which they pass, or the glory of the trees and
the changing beauty of the skies. With training, with developing awareness, you will find that you can pleasure yourself
much more fully in the everyday activities in which you
indulge.

"I will remember to pleasure myself as much as possible by
truly sensing during my waking hours." That simple sentence
will help you toward increasing your sensuality.

There are many books on sexual technique which are certainly helpful in many respects. But without the "sense"
awareness so important to sexual enjoyment, a new position
or new technique can do only so much for you. The exercises
in this chapter are designed to help increase your sensuality
and, therefore, your sexuality. Remember, the true joy of sex
is within your senses, your contact center. Truly SENSE the
experiences described.

Allow yourselves a minimum of one hour each time you begin to experience the following exercises. Better still, begin them when you have no time limit at all—on a lazy Sunday afternoon, say, or on vacation. Take the telephone off the hook, ignore the doorbell if it rings.

I ask that you *repeat* these exercises each time you work, adding to them as you wish. Be innovative and creative. Discover new ways to please each other and become aware of each other. You may wish to enhance the environment with candlelight, with pillows, with music. (Be careful that the music does not demand too much of your attention, that it only serves as background.)

SESSION I:

During your first session follow the instructions for exercises one through five. Do not skip any of the exercises and please be sure to do each one of them slowly, silently and seriously. By "seriously" I mean that although these are enjoyable experiences, they are also learning situations and are not to be treated lightly or jokingly. Have fun and enjoy, but do not undermine yourselves by negating the value of these experiences in any way.

If you are working alone, you will not be able to do exercise number one. However, the next exercises can and should be done by you. In exercises 2, 3, and 4, you will be exploring your own body. In exercise number 4, you will be recording your verbalizations on tape as you explore your body. You will note that there are several sentences in exercise 5 which may not be applicable to you working alone, or which you may wish to change slightly so that they are applicable. For example, change sentence number 7 from "Your face . . ." to "My face . . .".

Don't forget, by completing these sentences you will learn more about yourself and be able to use this new-found information for your own benefit in your everyday relationships.

EXPERIENCES FOR YOUR SENSES

(1.) Set an alarm clock for five minutes. Sit across from each other in as comfortable a position as possible. Look into each other's eyes without speaking until the alarm sounds. Do not speak at all. Do not stare at each other blankly. Really see. Examine each other's faces and expressions. Try to get messages from each other as to feelings and attitudes. Really see, not merely look. See what is in front of you.

(2.) At the end of the five minutes, still without speaking, take each other's right hand. Begin to explore that hand. Touch the fingers, the nails, the wrists. Pretend that you will have to recognize that hand in a crowd, so you must learn every inch of it. Become aware of the hair on the knuckles, the softness of the palm, the smoothness of the nails, the lines in the hand. Become aware of the veins, the indentations, the length of the fingers. Explore until you are sure you KNOW your partner's hand (or your own, if you are working alone).

(3.) Remove your clothing. One of you should lie down comfortably, on the back or stomach at first, whichever you prefer. Decide whether you want to keep your eyes open or closed as your partner explores your body with his hands and eyes. By exploring, you begin to know your partner's body thoroughly and completely. Touch the toes, in between each of them, the feet, the legs. Touch behind the knees, the insides of the thighs, the stomach, the chest, the shoulders. Be aware of the softness of some of the areas of the body, the hardness of other areas. Be aware of changes in the skin texture, the responses of your partner as you explore, and your own feelings as you look and touch. Examine the hands and arms, the face and head.

Thoroughly "learn" your partner's body. Do you see any birthmarks, any special indentation or place you especially like? Do you notice anything you have not noticed before? Did you touch a spot you realized your partner liked you to touch, or did not like you to touch? Do not miss any area of the body. (It is strongly suggested that you examine the genital areas as carefully and closely as you feel comfortable doing. A lack of knowledge of what the genital area looks like and all its parts is a hindrance to true sexual enjoyment.)

Turn your partner over and repeat the exploration. Be as aware as possible during the entire time. Watch your own reactions as you explore and watch your partner's reactions as you touch and look. Watch the body you are looking at. Really "see" what you are looking at. Be aware. DO NOT SPEAK.

Each of you take as much time as you want to for this exercise. Allow yourselves to learn as much as you can, to see as much as you can, and to feel as much as you can during this time.

Now repeat the above exercise, switching positions, letting your partner examine you as you examined him.

(4.) Repeat the above exercise, this time exploring each other simultaneously. It is suggested that, at this point, you turn on the tape recorder. Begin to record your verbalizations during this part of the exercise. (As I have mentioned, it is a good idea to record some of these exercises, and this is one of them.)

As you explore each other, speak to each other about your feelings. Tell each other if you like being touched "there" or "here" as you are touched. Tell each other how you feel about being looked at and examined. Speak to each other about your sensations in various areas of the body. Tell each other about the new areas you are finding on each other's bodies, the birthmarks you're seeing, the special places you find attractive. Speak as freely as you can about your sensations, your thoughts, your pleasure, or your discomfort, if any. Share with each other as much as you possibly can.

If you tape this, listen to the tape together after the experience. Share your thoughts about what you have said. It is an excellent learning technique to listen in on your experiences, to be able to share the feelings aroused and then be able to relive them again. Do try to tape as many of the suggested exercises as possible in this way.

(5.) Each of you take a pencil and paper. Without speaking to each other, write your responses to the following questions. When you have finished, exchange papers. Read them through carefully before you begin to discuss the experiences questioned. It is most important that you both agree to be honest and direct. Do not hold back. Too often sex problems stem from poor communication.

This questionnaire, like others in this book, helps to increase your communication, to establish links between you which may not have existed before on a verbal level. Use the information you have gained in reading your partner's questionnaire to try to increase his or her pleasure. This is another purpose of the questionnaire.

(1.) How do you FEEL right now? Try to answer in a few words.

(2.) List the best moments during the past few hours.

(3.) Complete: "I especially liked when———.

(4.) "I was embarrassed when———.

(5.) "I didn't like———.

(6.) "I learned that I———.

(7.) "Your face———.

(8.) "When I looked into your eyes during the first exercise———.

(9.) "When I looked into your eyes when exploring your face———.

(10.) "It is important to me that you———.

(11.) "It was especially hard not speaking when———.

(12.) "I was glad we were not allowed to speak when———.

(13.) "The types of touch I like best are———.

(14.) "Tell me that you———.

(15.) "Loving is———.

(16.) "It was good for me to———.

(17.) "I really wish that you had———.

(18.) "I was glad when———.

(19.) "I appreciate that you didn't———.

(20.) "What I really want you to know right now is———.

After reading each other's responses, take a few minutes to think about what you've just experienced. You've shared intimate contact with each other in a nonsexual situation. You've shared your feelings, your inhibitions, your dislikes, your likes. You've looked at each other and seen each other in very different ways for both of you. Your entire experience during this past hour or so has been new and unusual. Take a private moment to assess your own feelings right now. Be aware of what this has meant to you and what it will mean to your future relationship.

When you are ready to share your feelings about the responses to the questionnaire, and any other thoughts you may be having now, begin to discuss this with each other. Be as candid as possible. Remember that open communication is essential to true understanding and caring for each other. Honesty, about what you like and don't like, feel and want to feel, will help you in the exercises and experiences in this chapter and in the rest of this therapy program.

SESSION II:

The exercises in this session are designed primarily for couples, but if you are working alone, you can and should do the olfactory and tactile exercises. I suggest that you read all of the exercises through and learn them so that when you are with a partner, you can enjoy them.

Again, begin this session when you have at least an hour or more of private, uninterrupted time. During this session—and in the sessions which follow—I ask that you repeat the exercises you have done, adding to them as you go along. For example, at the beginning of this session, please repeat the direct eye contact, if only for a moment, when you first begin. Then explore each other's body for a moment or two. Feeling each other gently and slowly, relaxing each other. Remember all of the new information you now have about each other, touching each other where you most prefer to touch and be touched. Use the information you have obtained from the discussions, from listening to the tape recording, from the responses to the questionnaires, and your own increased awareness of yourself and of your partner.

During this session, you will need various types of materials. Have some soft types of fabric such as velvet, silk, pieces of fur, etc. Have a piece of cotton and a feather available, if possible. Have oil and powder available, too.

(6.) Begin this session by taking a bath or a shower together, after you have relaxed each other by looking at each other for a moment and touching each other, gently exploring and feeling each other's body. Wash each other gently and completely. Do not skip any areas of the body. This is a sensual experience. Do not dwell on the erotic areas or attempt stimulation of the clitoris, penis, or nipples. Pay EQUAL attention to all parts of the body. DO NOT PLAY FAVORITES. After washing each other, rinse each other free of soap, then dry each other thoroughly. Maintain eye contact as much as possible during this experience, not speaking but *feeling* what you are doing and having done to you. Speaking can detract from sensations, and you want to *sense* as intensely as possible.

(7.) Decide who wants to be massaged first. Begin the massage at the feet, gently rubbing and rotating each toe. Use your fingers and your hands along the base of the foot and the arch. Completely encircle the entire ankle, rubbing forcefully with strong upward strokes up the entire calf and thigh. Massage in circular motions with your fingers only, then with the palms of your hands. Knead the skin as you would dough. Use your knuckles as well. Pat with your palms. Go upward in arclike motions. Push the skin against the bones. Vary your strokes and your movements as you massage. Massage the buttocks and the back. Let your fingers follow the vertabrae of the spine one at a time, climbing the ladder of your partner's spine, going upward in circular motions. Massage the fingers, each one individually, the wrists and up the arms completely.

Don't skip any area of the body. Massaging, patting, rubbing. Push down with the full weight of your arms and hands to vary the stroke. Tap with your fingers at times, pat at others, rub gently and then with firmer strokes.

When you have massaged the entire body, from the feet up to the head, ask your partner to turn over so that you can massage the other side. Do the face and the head last. Massage all of the bones in the face gently using circular motions. Remember that speaking can detract from sensation so keep any talk to a minimum. Ask your partner to remain with his/her eyes closed. Smooth the skin around the eyes and the mouth. Gently pat the skull under the hair and rub in circular motions with your fingers only. When you have finished, pass your fingers and hands gently over the entire body several times, as if your fingers were feathers. Stop. Lie down next to your partner.

Remain silent for awhile. Allow the feelings and the sensations to seep into you. Enjoy the moment quietly. Think about your experience in giving the massage. Be aware of what you were feeling as you were giving your partner pleasure. Be aware of your sensations.

Some couples prefer to wait until the next session to reciprocate the massage. Others begin after a short rest, or even immediately. This is up to you. Do not speak about the experience immediately, though. Try to be aware of your feelings as quietly as possible before sharing them.

After you have both experienced a "dry" massage, do the same using warmed oil. Place a bottle of baby oil in a pot of hot water for five minutes or so. Put some oil on your hands every few minutes as you massage, following the same procedures described above.

Remain silent for a while after each experience, feeling your own feelings and learning to be as aware as you can of your sensations.

You may want to stop now and begin your next session with exercise number 8. This is up to you. Remember when you begin a new session to be as relaxed as possible and to allow enough time so that you won't feel pressured. Repeat exercise 6, if you begin a new session with exercise 8.

(8.) Explore each other's face with your eyes and with your fingertips. Touch and see. Smell and listen. Do not speak. Listen to your own sounds, your breathing, the sounds of the room, the sounds of the street. Rub your faces against each other, become aware of the hardness of the bones of the face by rubbing against each other. Find all of the soft spots, the crevices, the arches. Discover each other's face fully and completely. Look at each other deeply. DO NOT SPEAK. Be aware of what you are feeling as you are seeing your loved one and as your loved one sees you. Be as aware as you can of feelings of pleasure, discomfort, thoughts, whatever.

(9.) Please respond to the questions in exercise 5 again, this time keeping in mind that you are responding in reference to your reactions, feelings, thoughts, about exercises 6, 7, and 8. It is important that you write your responses first to help you to focus on them and to crystallize them in your mind and then to share them with your partner. Although you may have already discussed some of your reactions, by writing them you will find that it is easier to communicate your feelings and more will be shared in a fuller and deeper manner.

Again, exchange questionnaires and discuss your responses with each other. You will use these responses and this shared knowledge about each other to further enhance your mutual pleasure in future exercises and throughout your sensual and sexual life together.

In your future lovemaking, use any of these exercises which you especially like and enjoy. Be sure to always use some form of relaxation as you begin loving each other, so that you can fully enjoy the moment.

Be as innovative and creative as you care to or dare to, but be sure you pleasure and relax each other in some way EACH time. Discover new ways to please each other and to be pleased. Become as aware of each other as you can. You may wish to add bath oil to your bath together every once in a while, or bubble bath. You may want to soap yourselves completely—over your entire body—and then rub your bodies together, giving each other a "body massage." You can do this with oil as well, or create your own body massages.

While in the tub, you may wish to face each other and suck on each other's toes, taste each other's feet.

You may wish to try eating your favorite food from the body of your loved one. Try placing salad on your partner's stomach and eating it without using any utensils. Eat an entire meal without utensils from various parts of your partner's body. This is especially exciting when you eat something gooey, like chocolate pudding or custard, from each other's fingers or toes, or other body parts. Try it.

I suggested using various materials for some of these exercises. Let a feather glide over each other's bodies. Stroke each other with a piece of soft cotton, or fur, or silk, or velvet. Rub each other with powder. Put various odors on pieces of cotton and smell them, truly sensing the odor. Develop your olfactory sense as much as possible. Smell each other's body, and begin to enjoy the pleasure of smelling the sweet clean skin of your beloved.

Even if you are working alone, you can enjoy these experiences. Try them. Give yourself these pleasures—bathing yourself, stroking yourself, smelling yourself and eating foods from your own body. Intensify your own sensuality in this way, so that you can share it later with a partner.

Speak in various tones of voice. Use different types of language. Use baby talk, foreign language phrases. Excite and stimulate with your voice and your choice of words. Use a tape recorder, so that you can experience your own voice and hear the changes in it.

Be aware of what your partner is feeling as you are offering these various stimuli. Share your feelings and your thoughts with each other. One couple discovered that the woman had orgasm when listening to certain verbal expressions. When her partner graphically described what he was feeling and sensing as he made love to her, this excited her to the point of orgasm. Have your partner read turn-on literature or say "forbidden words" to you. See if you are especially sensitive to auditory stimuli.

When sharing your feelings about sexual experiences with each other, you are opening up doors of communication which may have been closed for too long a time. When inhibitions are decreased, pleasures are greatly increased. The sexual and emotional life of couples improves greatly by experiencing these sensual activities together and by sharing each other's feelings as fully and completely as possible.

There are techniques throughout this program designed to help you toward more open and free communication. As you learn to speak WITH each other, not merely to each other, you will realize how very important the questionnaires are. Please be sure to utilize them to the fullest. Sharing is loving, and sharing cannot be without honesty and trust.

The exercises in this chapter are sensual and will excite you to feelings of sexuality. When done faithfully and with a feeling of warmth and love for each other and for yourselves, you will develop and intensify your sensuality and your sexuality. Maintain this sensual feeling. It's yours to keep with your "Help Yourself Sex Therapy" program. Enjoy it.

CHAPTER 7

Relaxation and Image-Making

THE word sexuality brings a great many mental pictures to mind. Some see sexuality as looks: a hulking, broadshouldered, slim-hipped male, a large-bosomed, long-haired sultry female. Others see sexuality as a less obvious manifestation of the sense of sex. Men who are really MEN, or women who are really WOMEN, are sexy, they have sexuality. But what is a man who is really a MAN? A woman who is really a WOMAN? What is sexuality? Whatever it is, it is personal, individual, and extremely difficult to describe in general terms.

Sexuality, in the context of this book, is the ability to experience physical sensations and emotional freedom completely and fully. A sexual being feels sensations and stimulations intensely and with a great deal of joy and pleasure. A sexual being is free to involve himself, or herself, with abandon and openness in experiences of the flesh. Sexuality is the open road, the magic carpet, the Apollo I to physical and emotional pleasure.

There are methods which aid and direct us toward these feelings. *You Can Be Your Own Sex Therapist* has developed such methods, geared toward getting you in touch with your own sexuality. Everyone is a sexual human being. When we are born, we have the ability to experience equally delightful pleasure all over our bodies. As we mature, we are trained out of these responses.

We can relearn how to be sexual and how to respond to various stimulations in the intensely physical and emotional way which we deserve. This learning has nothing to do with our looks. It has nothing to do with our age, our financial status, our gender, or where we live. Each and every one of

57

us—regardless of background, physical appearance, age, color or creed—has not only the inherent, God-given right to pleasure, but also the ability to relearn to experience pleasure intensely and fully.

Relaxation and image-making increase your sense perception and help you to learn to be aware of your bodily sensations. This awareness is necessary for developing your sexuality.

One of the most difficult factors in increasing sexuality is attitude. You can understand why this is so. If a person has certain restrictive attitudes about the pleasures of the flesh, or inhibitions about certain types of physical behavior, then it is very difficult to create a free and easy feeling of joy and excitement about sex. There may be guilt, or distaste, due to childhood experiences, your parents' attitudes, your religious background.

I can say only that everyone is entitled to pleasure. Sexual pleasure is one of the most intense and joyful experiences in the world. When there is caring, warmth, and true feeling between two people, the act of love is a moment of beauty and perfection.

By reading this book, feeling the flavor of loving feelings toward sex, realizing the limitless boundaries of delight which can be derived from happy sex and accepting the fact that you DESERVE to experience this delight, your attitudes will, hopefully, be directed toward a more open, uninhibited form of sexuality.

Another difficult factor to deal with is your own self-image. If you see yourself as a sexual being, you will *be* a sexual being. If you feel that your body is not right, your face is wrong, or your age keeps you from erotic pleasure, then this is how it will be.

You have only to read some of the great literature, or biographies of famous persons, to know that looks and age are unimportant. The Duchess of Windsor was past 30 when King Edward fell in love with her and abdicated his throne for her. Elizabeth Barrett Browning was crippled but totally adored and worshiped by Robert. At the prime of her life, Jackie Kennedy married Aristotle Onassis, although he was considerably older.

All of these people were loved for much more than merely physical appearance. I could go on and on with proof that there are people who have a certain sexual energy and charm which goes far above and beyond any attraction formed merely on looks.

There are situations in your own neighborhood, your own family, your own office, where couples have gotten together to love and to enjoy their lives regardless of the fact that they were "beyond the age of love or sex," "too fat or too ugly for that sort of thing," and all of the other silly stereotypes that go with who is "supposed" to love and be sexual and who is not supposed to be loved. This is one more attitude that should be jettisoned. You DESERVE to be a sexual being. Feel that way and it will be that way. The way you feel is both a result and a cause of your behavior.

The entire sense of sexuality, the sense of how you feel about yourself is crucial to how others will feel about you. You can learn to exercise the kind of control over your mind and your body, so that you will be closer to who and what and how you want to be. There is a new science called biofeedback, which has proven—with the use of electronic equipment—that your mind can exercise control over your body. When your body feels good, when it is relaxed and calm, your behavior will be so much more pleasurable and contented. When your mind is calm, quieted from all of the anxieties, fears and inhibitions which you may have regarding sex, you can enjoy your sexual life so much more.

Biofeedback, the science of controlling your physiology with your mind, has shown that you can learn to "quiet" your mind, relax your body, even control your thoughts as you maintain a "quiet mind."

When your ceful green field, electronic iilled with worry and fear, you cannot enjoy any pleasant experience or stimulation which may be occuring. Tension is not something which comes in from the outside world. It is a feeling which you create mostly in your own body, out of your thoughts. As you feel that mental tension, your muscles begin to tense and you begin to feel physical tension.

When you are doing breathing exercises or creating images of blue skies and a peaceful green field, electronic instru-

ments such as the electromyograph and the electroen-
cephalograph, indicate that your muscles relax, your perspi-
ration rate lowers, and your brain waves become much slower.
This scientific proof of the mind's ability to control physiological processes is comparatively recent. Only within the past
twelve years, has biofeedback become more and more sophis-
ticated in using this knowledge. For example, people are
learning to lower their blood pressure, rid themselves of mi-
graine headaches, develop muscular control in formerly
atrophied muscles and much more.

The point is that you can control your physiological state
through various exercises and techniques which help to quiet
your mind and thereby quiet and relax your body. This
"quieting" of your body and mind is, in actuality, teaching you
to relax, to be free of tightness, tension, fears and inhibitions,
which are negative forces.

Specific physical exercises are most helpful when muscles
are tense and when there is a general tired, "tight" feeling in
the body. I have included such exercises and you can use them
as frequently as you wish. Actually, you should use at least one
of these relaxation exercises each time you begin a "Help
Yourself Sex Therapy" session. Repeat this exercise as often
as you need to, until you really feel your mind and your body
relaxing, releasing you from all tension and thought.

I suggest that you tape-record the following so that you can
listen to it without interruption. If you are working alone, this
is especially important. If you are working with a partner, you
can read the exercise to each other or listen to the tape
together.

BEGIN READING HERE:

Place yourself in as relaxed a position as possible, lying or
sitting. Do NOT cross your arms or legs. Be as loose as you can
be. Do NOT wear tight clothing, belts, jewelry, ties and so on.
If you feel anything that is tight, remove it now.

Before you begin, try to feel if there is any tenseness in your
body. Express aloud if any of the following muscles feels tight
to you:

Are your feet tight? (Allow time after each question for the
response.)

Breathe in and tighten your feet muscles.
Breathe out and let your feet muscles go, let them relax.
Are your thighs tight?
Breathe in and tighten your thigh muscles.
Breathe out and let your thigh muscles go, let them relax.
Is your stomach tight?
Breathe in and tighten your stomach muscles.
Breathe out and let your stomach muscles go.
Is your chest tight?
Breathe in and tighten your chest muscles.
Breathe out and let your chest muscles go, let them relax.
Are your shoulder muscles tight?
Breathe in and tighten your shoulder muscles.
Breathe out and let your shoulder muscles go, let them relax.
Are your arm muscles tight?
Breathe in and tighten your arm muscles.
Breathe out and let your arm muscles go, let them relax.
Are your hand muscles tight?
Breathe in and tighten your hand muscles.
Breathe out and let your hand muscles go, let them relax.
Is your back tight?
Breathe in and tighten your back muscles.
Breathe out and let your back muscles go, let them relax.
Is your neck tight?
Breathe in and tighten your neck muscles.
Breathe out and let your neck muscles go, let them relax.
Is your face tight?
Breathe in and tighten your face muscles.
Breathe out and let your face muscles go, let them relax.
Take a deep breath and tighten all of your muscles. Let the air out, letting go of the tightness in your muscles. Let it all out. Let it all relax. Again, breathe in and tighten your entire body. Hold your breath and continue to tighten all of your muscles. Let the air out, letting go of all of the tightness in your muscles. Let it all out. Let it all relax.
Take a deep breath and hold your breath for approximately 15 seconds. Tighten your body as you breathe in. Tighten your arms, your legs, your face, your chest, your

buttocks—very, very tight. NOW—let go. . . . let out your breath with a sound. Make as loud a sound as you can as you let out your breath.

Again, take a very deep breath, tightening your entire body as you breathe in. Tighten your face, your hands, your arms, your legs, your stomach. TIGHT, TIGHT, TIGHT. Hold your breath. HOLD, HOLD, HOLD. Let go with as loud a sound as you can make. As you let the air out, let the sound out.

Do this again slowly, and at your own pace. As you let the air out, let the loud sound out.

Do this again slowly, and at your own pace. Breathe in deeply. Hold your breath in and tighten your entire body. TIGHT, TIGHT, TIGHT. HOLD, HOLD, HOLD. LET GO—let out a sound, as loud as you can.

Wait a few moments as you allow yourself to feel the sensations of relaxation and peacefulness throughout your mind and body. Share with each other and discuss your feelings now. If you are working alone, speak aloud, preferably taping your responses so that you will have them to listen to and learn from.

If you are working with a partner, it is also good to tape your conversations after each exercise. Tell about the parts of your body which you are more aware of than other parts and which parts are now more relaxed. Do you feel any difference in your body? Is there a difference in temperature, in lightness, in tightness? Was it easy for you to make a loud sound, or did you have difficulty really shouting out and letting go?

Become as aware as possible of every one of your sensations. Did you smell the air more fully as you concentrated on the breathing in? Did you have any images in your mind?

Share your thoughts and feelings, asking each other questions and communicating fully about this exercise. If alone, try to delve deeply into yourself and speak aloud about all of these sensations.

Another form of relaxation which I use a great deal and which I feel is very beneficial in *You Can Be Your Own Sex Therapist* is known as "image-making." This exercise will help you to learn to create images in your mind. Again, I suggest that you record this exercise on a tape recorder so that you can listen to it later. Also, you will have it ready whenever you want to use it, and not need to repeat it each time.

Place yourself in as relaxed a position as possible. Close your eyes. I would like you to imagine that there is a tube going down your body from behind your nose, down past your mouth, throat, chest and stomach—all the way down to your genital area. Picture this tube as clearly as you can in your mind's eye.

We are going to imagine that we can bring air down this tube, completely clearing it, making our breathing calmer and easier.

Begin now. Bring air in through your nostrils, down to the point in the tube just behind your nose.

Try to see the air as it comes down the tube.

Imagine the air swirling around inside the tube behind your nose.

Watch the color of the air as it goes in. Watch the color of the air as it goes out.

Bring the air in through your nostrils, all the way down to behind your mouth.

Watch the air circle around inside, swirling around.

Let it out. Watch the color as it comes out.

Bring the air down again, this time all the way down to your throat.

Feel the ease with which it comes into your body, relaxing and energizing you. Air is energy.

Breathing properly is life-giving energy.

Allow the air to swirl around inside the tube from the top of your nose to your throat.

Let it out slowly and gradually.

Now bring the air down as far as your chest, between your breasts.

Allow the air to swirl down the tube, watching it as it goes down, relaxing and easing you.

Let it out slowly and easily.

Watch the color as it comes out of your nostrils.

This time, bring the air down to your belly button.

Watch it flow down from the top of your nose to your belly button.

Become aware of any tightness the air may be experiencing inside the tube. Allow the air to loosen any tightness.

Allow it to come down smoothly and gradually.

Let it out. Watch the air as it leaves your body.

Does the color change as it comes in and as it leaves?

Watch the air inside the tube in your mind's eye.

Bring the air down to your belly button again.

Watch it ease its way down.

Let it out, watching the color of the air.

Become aware of any images you may be viewing in your mind's eye.

Don't follow the images or think about them. Merely become aware of them.

Bring the air in again, this time all the way down to the genital area.

Let it swirl around the base of the tube, relaxing your genital area.

Let it out slowly and gradually.

Watch the color as it comes out.

Repeat this again. Bring the air down, slowly and easily, all the way down, past your nose, your mouth, your throat, your chest, your belly button, all the way to the genital area.

Watch the air swirling upward as it leaves your body.

Watch the color. Become aware of any color changes.

Watch yourself and become aware of how you are feeling now. Without opening your eyes, when you are ready, describe the feelings in your body. Share your feelings with each other. Tape record this discussion if you can.

These exercises are designed specifically to relax you and to put your mind and body into a receptive and calm state. You should do at least one of them each time you begin a lovemaking session. Unless you are fully relaxed, feeling good and loose, it is very difficult to follow any of the exercises. Certainly it is very difficult to enjoy them fully. The exercises—as the entire program in this book—are pleasant, fun and exciting in addition to being learning experiences. To get the most from the program, please follow it exactly. Choose a relaxation exercise and use it each time you begin your "Help Yourself Sex Therapy."

You may select a relaxation exercise from another book, or use one which you develop yourself and which you know works for you. Just be sure that you do something that relaxes you, frees you from negative thoughts and worries, and gives you a feeling of looseness.

Since image-making is vital to sexual pleasure for many reasons, I'd like to give you one more exercise to help you to increase your image-making abilities. Please use this especially if you had difficulty in "seeing the images" created by the first image-making exercise.

Image-making is used during the sexual experience as a "turn-on." It helps you to stimulate yourself sexually, to envision your fantasies as clearly as possible, to become as sexually creative as you can, and to use your mental capacities to the fullest. Through image-making, you can free your mind of negative thoughts, free your body of tension and use all of your capacities fully.

Tape record this exercise as well. Speak slowly and calmly, in as melodic a voice as possible. Lie down, as relaxed and loose as possible. Take a few deep breaths to become as relaxed as possible.

Imagine that you are walking toward a staircase.

In your mind's eye, watch yourself as you come closer to the staircase.

The staircase has a banister, along the left side.

See the banister clearly and completely. It is a yellow banister.

See the texture of the banister. See the design of the banister.

Take one step upward, placing your right foot on the first step of the staircase.

Place your left hand on the yellow banister.

Raise your left foot and place it on the first step of the staircase.

See the red carpeting on the first step. See the yellow banister.

Place your right foot on the next step. See the green carpeting on the second step of the staircase.

Look back at the red step. Look down at the green step.

Feel the yellow banister under your left hand.

Place your right foot on the next step. Keep your hand on the yellow banister.

Place your left foot on the next step. See the blue carpeting on the third step of the staircase.

Look back at the second, green step.

Look back at the first, red step.

Feel the yellow banister beneath your left hand.

Place your right foot on the next step. Keep your hand on the yellow banister.

Place your left foot on the next step. See the orange carpeting on the fourth step of the staircase.

Look back at the third, blue step.

Look back at the second, green step.

Look back at the first, red step.

Feel the yellow banister beneath your left hand.

You are almost to the top of the staircase. You have one more step to go.

Place your right foot on the last step. Keep your hand on the yellow banister.

Place your left foot on the last step. See the white carpeting on the last step of the staircase.

Look back at the fourth, orange step.

Look back at the third, blue step.

Look back at the second, green step.

Feel the yellow banister beneath your left hand.

Begin to walk back down the staircase.

Stand on the fourth step—the orange step.

Stand on the third step—the blue step.

Stand on the second step—the green step.

Stand on the first step—the red step.

Let go of the yellow banister.

Step off the staircase.

Remain still for a while. Enjoy the feeling of quietness and relaxation. When you are ready, try to become aware of the usefulness of this technique.

Allow a few minutes of silence on the tape for quiet moments. (Continue to tape this section of the exercise as well, so that when you experience it, it will flow easily without any need to stop.)

Could you visualize the colors? Could you feel the texture of the banister? Could you feel the carpeting beneath your feet? Could you see yourself as you climbed the steps? Could you feel your legs as they rose, one at a time, from step to step?

Can you imagine increasing your image-making ability so that you can actually envision, actually see, a sexual fantasy—a face, a position, a behavior which can turn you on and give you pleasure? Can you imagine using this skill to increase creativity and originality in your sexual behaviors? Try to envision your own image, make your own scene. See yourself as you would most like to be and experience what you would most like to experience. Feel the joy of the image and the joy of the sensations drawn out by the image.

I realize that these are new types of experiences for most of you and that it is sometimes quite difficult to allow yourself to relax, to experience yourself in this way, and even more difficult to share your feelings about your bodily sensations and your levels of awareness. But I also know how important it is that you achieve a sense of self-awareness and an ability to relax.

Some couples find it easier to use the questions I presented above as a guide as they discuss this exercise. During their discussion, they write the answers to these questions first, then they read the answers to each other. They report that they find this the easiest approach to more free-and-easy discussion. You may want to try it.

Whatever you decide, be sure to share as much as you are aware of and be sure to truly watch your thoughts and your body to intensify your awareness. Please follow the technique as closely as you can. Only that way will you gain the most from my experience and knowledge. If you are working alone, record or write your responses, learn as much about yourself as possible.

Here is another exercise which is both relaxing and also helpful in training the image-making process. You can pre-tape this exercise or read it to each other. Allow about fifteen minutes to complete it.

Begin by placing yourself in as relaxed and comfortable a position as possible. Be sure you do not have your legs crossed or your arms folded. Be as loose as you can.

Breathe in and out slowly for a few minutes, becoming aware of your breathing. Relax as you breathe in, saying, "Air is coming in," and as you breathe out, saying, "Air is going out." Repeat these words slowly, in rhythm with your breathing.

Breathe in and out at your own pace, using the air and your concentration to ease your tensions. Empty your mind of all thoughts. Allow your mind to be at rest. Allow your mind to be quiet. A quiet mind is a joyful, peacefully beautiful experience. Allow your mind to be quiet.

Allow the air to relax and calm your body. Remember, air is energy. Proper breathing is energizing and relaxing.

Continue to breathe quietly in and out.

Begin to create a scene in your mind's eye. Begin to see a staircase in front of you. Watch yourself as you walk toward the staircase and place one foot on the first step.

The step is covered with a bright red carpet. The carpet is thick and soft beneath your foot. Bring your other foot up to the step.

Allow the redness of the carpet to fill your mind's eye. See the red step clearly and vividly. Begin to imagine that the red begins to flow through your body.

Allow the red to come up through your feet into your body. Merely watch the flow of red as it eases up your legs, your trunk, your arms, and head.

Become aware of this scene in your mind and of the feelings in your body. Watch this carefully and intently. When you are ready, take another step and watch your foot as it touches a blue step.

The step is a vivid, deep blue. The carpet is soft and thick. You can feel the springiness in your step as you bring your other foot up to this vivid, deep blue step.

Allow the color to fill your mind's eye. See it as clearly as you can. Watch the vivid, deep blue as it flows up your body, through your feet, your legs, your trunk, your arms, and your head.

Allow the blue to permeate your mind's eye. Allow the softness of the carpet to follow the blue, creating a feeling of softness and yielding in your body. Relax. Concentrate on the blueness.

Now take another step. This time the step is a bright yellow. Allow your feet to touch the bright yellow and watch the yellow travel upwards toward your head. Allow the softness of the carpet to flow upward permeating your body. Watch the image being created in your mind. Watch the yellow and the softness as it travels throughout your body. Relax, watching the image as it is created in your mind's eye.

Take one last step. This time the step is green, the green of the grass on a bright summer day. A clear, sharp green. Allow yourself to feel the green of the step under your feet. Feel the softness and the depth of the carpet as you sink into the green, as if on soft, thick grass. Allow the green to travel through your body, permeating your body with green—bright, vivid green. Relax, watching the flow of green.

Continue to breathe in and out slowly and at your own pace. Repeat again: "Air is coming in . . . air is going out."

Don't allow any other thoughts. If images come into your mind, allow them to come, but don't follow them. Just watch them emerge and flow on by, as though a series of clouds were passing in front of you. Continue repeating: "Air is coming in . . . air is going out." Keep your mind quiet.

Share this experience with each other after you have both created the images.

Were you able to see the colors clearly?

Were you able to allow your imagination to flow so that you could see the color permeating your body?

Did you feel the softness of the carpet flow through your body?

How do you feel now, after experiencing this image-making technique? Share your thoughts and your feelings. Tape-record your responses, if you can.

Relaxation and image-making are most important aids to a sexual experience which is more gratifying and fulfilling. Imagining seems to relieve many of the tensions and fears surrounding sex. It allows the body to respond more fully to various stimulations.

The more sensations you can experience, the more you can be aware of and in tune with your senses, the fuller and more complete your sexual experiences will be.

Practice these exercises until they become a part of you and you can use them at your will. The more proficient you become in using them, the more you will gain from them . . . and the more joy you will have.

CHAPTER 8

Know Your Body: Sexual Exercises
Know Your Mind:
Image-Making Exercises

Do you know if your nipples are hard, without touching them or looking at them? Think carefully. Do you really know for sure? Would you bet on your awareness of this? If you are a male do you know—*really know*—if you have an erection unless you look at or touch your penis? If female, do you know if your vagina is moist? Do you have to touch yourself, or be touched, before you are sure that your vagina is or is not moist?

These questions are very often answered no. At first you may think you are aware of these physiological phenomena. But when you really concentrate, you'll realize that awareness of these physical manifestations comes through the sense of touch or sight.

It is very difficult to be fully aware of your body, but it certainly is possible to learn more about your body and its physical changes than you now know. Your first step in developing this awareness is to begin with a very relaxed and quiet mind and body. Therefore, before you begin any of the exercises in this chapter, quiet yourself and relax, using the first breathing exercise in Chapter 7. Add any other relaxation exercises you may like. When you are as relaxed and quiet as possible, try this experiment:

Shake your hands vigorously, as hard as you can for twenty seconds. STOP. Feel the sensation in your fingers—without touching them. Do you feel them tingling? Do you feel a kind of vibration in them? Do they feel warmer to you? If you do not answer yes to all of these questions, shake your hands again, harder. Do you feel these sensations now?

This is a simple exercise which quickly and easily demonstrates how your body responds to stimulation. Regardless of the type of stimulation, the body will respond in some way. This was vigorous exercise and the response was obvious. You may have noticed that there are many changes the body can go through when stimulated, many of which are almost imperceptible.

Try this exercise, which is much more subtle. Be as relaxed as you can before you begin. Have your partner read this exercise to you, or tape it so that you can both do it together. (This exercise should take at least twenty minutes.)

Remove your clothing, lying nude and relaxed, close your eyes and let your mind go blank.

Picture a white screen in front of you—empty, white, blank.

Begin to see your own body on the screen.

Look at your legs. See them as clearly as you can. (Pause: 30 seconds)

Feel how your legs are feeling now as you look at them. (Pause: 30 seconds)

Look at your body from the waist down.

See the hips, the genital area, the thighs, the legs.

Feel how this part of your body is feeling as you look at it. (Pause: 30 seconds)

Look at your breasts or chest.

Feel how this part of your body is feeling as you look. (Pause: 30 seconds)

Look at your face . . . what is your expression?

Feel how your face is feeling as you look at it. (Pause: 30 seconds)

Look at your entire body. Can you see the whole person?

Feel how you are feeling as you look at yourself. (Pause: 30 seconds)

Begin again. This time, imagine someone you feel very close to, someone you care for very much is looking at you on the screen. This person is looking at your legs. (Pause: 15 seconds)

How are your feelings in your legs as this person looks at

you? Become aware if there is any change in the feelings in your legs as the person looks at you. (Pause: 30 seconds)

This person is looking at your body from the waist down.

Look at the hips, the genital area, the thighs, the legs.

Become aware of how this part of your body is feeling as this person looks at you. (Pause: 30 seconds)

Are there any changes in your body feelings now?

This person is looking at your breasts or chest. (Pause: 30 seconds)

Feel how this part of your body is feeling as this person is looking. (Pause: 30 seconds)

This person is looking at your face.

What is your expression?

Become aware of any change in your expression. (Pause: 15 seconds)

Your entire body is being looked at.

Become aware of any parts of your body which feel different than other parts. (Pause: 30 seconds)

Watch everything through your own eyes again. (Pause: 15 seconds)

Look at your face. (Pause: 15 seconds)

Look at your body. (Pause: 15 seconds)

Look at your genital area. (Pause: 15 seconds)

Look at your legs. (Pause: 15 seconds)

Try to watch your feelings. Are you experiencing any sensations which are different. Are your sensations changing? (Pause: 30 seconds)

Become as aware as you can.

Is your expression changed?

Do you feel more comfortable looking at yourself, than when the person was looking at you? (Pause: 15 seconds)

Which parts of your body felt different and which parts felt the same?

Remain very quiet. Try not to think. Feel your body. Feel any tingles, any tension, any pulsations. (Pause: 15 seconds)

Feel the temperature on your face, in your hands, in your genital area.

Tune in to your sensations. Be as aware as you can. Watch. Feel. Remain quiet as long as you want to.

Discuss your reactions with your partner, and all your

responses to this exercise. Verbalize any feelings you may be having at this moment.

Who was the person you chose to look at you? Was it your partner, a parent, a grandparent?

Were your feelings different or were they the same? Did you experience any embarrassment?

Did you like the way your body looked?

Did the person like the way your body looked? Did you wish you could change anything? Did you become tense at any point? When?

What do you know about your own body's reaction now that you might not have known before? Could you actually feel sensations, changes, physical manifestations of feelings such as shame or pleasure? How did your body feel as it responded to your emotional feelings?

Try to tune in to all of these questions. As you do, you'll be tuning in to the sensations of your body, training yourself to be with your feelings as much as possible.

In training yourself to be in touch with your feelings, to be aware of the sensations aroused by this fantasy, you are becoming familiar with your own sense of yourself and of your body. This awareness is the first step toward being comfortable with the feelings you have about your body. The more aware you can be, the more comfortable you will be. The more comfortable you are, the freer you will be. The freer you are, the more enjoyment you will feel during the sexual and sensual experiences of your life.

If you become self-conscious, you can benefit from the desensitization exercises in Chapter 19.

This may seem like an oversimplified explanation, but you will see as you progress in this program, that awareness is an essential step toward the amelioration of problems and toward control of any situation you choose to control.

Knowledge about yourself is essential. These exercises— through fantasy, through open and honest discussion after each exercise, through your increasing use of your senses— will bring you to greater and greater awareness of yourself:

KNOW YOUR MIND—SEXUAL FANTASIES

This exercise will help you to focus on your own vision of

yourself as a sexual being. You will be able to see yourself as you think others see you, feel yourself as you feel others feel about you and be aware of your bodily sensations as you experience these thought-provoking images.

With the use of this exercise, you will be able to create your own fantasies, tailor-made to your own needs and desires. Remember that your goal is to become as aware as possible of what you feel about yourself, your body, your sexual activities. You want to be able to visualize this in fantasy. You want to fantasize about what others feel about you as you perform certain sexual and sensual acts. You want to be aware of your physical sensations as you imagine what others are feeling about you and as you participate in sexual activities within your fantasy.

Think about the goals of this exercise as you read through the questions. Read them all through carefully before you begin to answer them. If you are working with a partner, each of you should answer the questions separately first, then share the answers with the other. If you are working alone, answer the questions to learn as much as you can about yourself.

During the testing stage of *You Can Be Your Own Sex Therapist,* some couples said they did not want to answer all of the questions. You may feel this way too. Before you begin the exercise, you should decide if there *are* any questions you do not choose to answer. If there are, tell your partner that you do not choose to answer question X or Y, or whatever. You should not explain anything. You do not need a reason for not wanting to answer any of the questions. Accept from each other whatever decision is reached about answering or not answering any of these questions.

This is an essential point. You must learn to respect each other's privacy. Your partner may decide not to answer X and Y; you may not wish to answer A and B. This decision is to be respected—no questions asked. Respond only to the questions you want to and share the answers to these questions. However, I do suggest that in private, on your own time, each of you answer the questions you skipped and discover what it was about them that made you reluctant to respond. Discover this for yourself; the information will be only for you.

Now, proceed to answer those questions you've BOTH agreed to respond to:

(1.) What do fantasies mean to you?

(2.) Is there anything negative about having a fantasy?

(3.) Can your body respond to the thoughts in your mind as you fantasize?

(4.) Can these bodily responses help you in any way to become more aware of your bodily sensations? If yes, how? If no, how do you know?

(5.) Do you have sexual fantasies during the day? Is there a "regular" storyline?

(6.) Would you like to create a fantasy to help your partner become aware of his/her bodily sensations?

(7.) Would you share the fantasy with him/her?

(8.) Which of your senses are you least aware of?

(9.) What types of fantasies can help you to become more aware of these senses?

(10.) What would you most want to feel right now?

(11.) How can fantasy help you to feel this sensation?

(12.) Write down a fantasy which will help your sense of smell.

(13.) Write down a fantasy which will help develop your sense of muscle relaxation.

(14.) Write down a fantasy which will develop your sense of taste.

(15.) Can your sense of touch be developed through fantasy, so it can increase your enjoyment of sex?

(16.) What is your favorite sexual fantasy?

(17.) What is your most unusual sexual fantasy?

(18.) Imagine yourself performing a "crazy" sexual act.

(19.) Get yourself as excited as possible by visualizing something. What is it?

(20.) Watch yourself make love. Feel the sensations. Watch the activity. What do you do? How do you do it? Watch the entire lovemaking from beginning to end.

These questions are difficult ones and will take a great deal of your time and effort. Remember, it is most important that you develop your awareness of your body and how your body feels when it is stimulated in various ways. Fantasy is one of the most rewarding methods to expand your horizons.

Here is a questionnaire as completed by one woman in "Help Yourself Sex Therapy." She found that although it took her some time to complete her answers, she found them infinitely helpful:

SAMPLE RESPONSES

(1.) What do fantasies mean to you?

I never really thought about it, I think of them as daydreams, really.

(2.) Is there anything negative about having a fantasy?

I feel I'd rather do it, than fantasize it.

(3.) Can your body respond to the thoughts in your mind as you fantasize?

Not really, it's hard for me to think of a feeling and feel it.

(4.) Can these bodily responses help you in any way in terms of becoming more aware of your bodily sensations?

If I knew what was happening, I guess I could then learn more about my body and how it responds, so I guess with practice I can learn what's happening.

If yes, how? If no, how do you know?

If you could tell me if my body is responding when you read a fantasy to me, then I would become aware of it, and then I think I'd be able to tell it the next time. (Example: Her partner did tell her that he noticed her nipples hardening as he read a fantasy which he'd written about two men and a woman making love.)

(5.) Do you have sexual fantasies during the day? Is there a "regular" storyline?

I always wish I was being lavished with hugging and kissing and gentle loving.

(6.) Would you like to create a fantasy to help your partner to become aware of his/her bodily sensations?

Yes, I would like to have the fun of writing a fantasy and then sharing it.

(7.) Would you share the fantasy with him/her?

Yes, I already answered that. The sharing would be most of the fun.

(8.) Which of your senses are you least aware of?

I really think I've tuned out smells.

(9.) What types of fantasies can help you to become more aware of these senses?

Maybe hearing about flowers, perfumes, fish or coffee. You know, strong-smelling things.

(10.) What would you most want to feel right now?

I would like to feel good inside me and not feel that I'm tense and rigid a lot of the time—not really feeling but thinking a lot, and nervous because of my thoughts.

(11.) How can fantasy help you to feel this sensation?

Oh, a lot. The relaxation fantasies are really good for me and I'd like to do them more often, even make up some that I could use often, in my own head, to relax me.

(12.) Write down a fantasy which will help develop your sense of smell.

I just did, number 9.

(13.) Write down a fantasy which will develop your sense of muscle relaxation.

If you would talk to me about different muscles in my body, and let me imagine that I'm using them, or relaxing them, and then see if it works—like some of the relaxation exercises do—then I think I'd tune in more to my insides and muscles and stuff.

(14.) Write down a fantasy which will develop your sense of taste.

Oh, talk to me about food, all kinds—chocolate, ice cream, spaghetti, pizza, whatever. As I'm writing, I think I'm aware of a bodily sensation. My mouth really felt wetter, as if it was "watering." Is that possible?

(15.) Can your sense of touch be developed through fantasy, so it can improve your enjoyment of sex?

Yes, I think so. I enjoy being touched so much, but I'm not really sure of what I'm touching, and I think if I could tune in more to textures and tones, I'd have more fun.

(16.) What is your favorite sexual fantasy?

I always fantasize that I am being "done to," that my lover is loving me, licking me, kissing me and hugging me and not asking for anything back.

(17.) What is your most unusual sexual fantasy?

I guess it's that I'll be the wildest, sexiest, most sought-after hooker in the world—completely free of all inhibitions, running around naked, seducing every male in sight.

(18.) Imagine yourself performing a "crazy" sexual act.

Oh boy, almost everything strange is "crazy" to me. Okay, here I am with two men. I'm having oral sex with one. I'm doing it to him—and the other one is stroking my body as he is having intercourse with me. And, oh, yes, the one I'm having oral sex with, he's massaging me and telling me he loves me over and over.

(19.) Get yourself as excited as you possibly can by visualizing something.

The first thing that comes to my mind is my body being stroked for hours and hours, just being done to, and loving every moment of it.

(20.) Watch yourself make love. Feel the sensations. Watch the activity. What do you do? How do you do it? Watch the entire lovemaking from beginning to end.

Now that's heavy. I can see it as I do it now. He touches me a little, he licks my nipples. I touch him, maybe kiss his penis for a while, and then we have intercourse. But I can see it as I'd like it too. Much more touching and kissing. Much more oral sex. Again a lot of stroking as I lie there writhing in pleasure and ecstasy. He massages and loves me with his hands, with his tongue, with his body, rubbing himself against me over and over. I do the same with him. We touch for hours, stroking and loving each other. We have oral sex, first just him to me, and then just me to him, and then together. We penetrate after a lot of this, and we move slowly and gently, hardly moving at all. I do a lot of moving and screaming. I wish I could really do this. I'd love to really move and make noise.

This woman's partner was able to respond to these answers in a great many ways. He learned a lot about what she would like him to do and about what she really wanted. She also had to focus on various matters which she hadn't really thought about before. That helped her to raise her level of awareness. She discovered what really turned her on and was able not only to fantasize about it, but really to experience it as well.

This questionnaire will help *you* to tune in to *your* private needs and wishes. Focusing on the answers to these questions forces you to look consciously at various stimuli in your life, at those sensations which are most stimulating, at those senses which you've neglected for too long and at what you can do to enjoy all of your senses.

It also helps you to look at what fantasy, imagination, and

creativity can do for you and to discover how truly creative and unique you are. We are all much more talented than we believe we are. These questions will bring this creativity out of you in deeply constructive ways. You can work with all of this information to improve your sexual satisfaction, just as others have.

After you've both completed the questionnaire, share your answers and discuss them with each other. Tape this discussion so that you can learn from your remarks by listening to them again. Try to fulfill each other's requests, not just once, but by referring to these responses often. Continue trying to raise each other's levels of bodily awareness by repeating the requests you made of each other, possibly changing them as you become more aware of your own needs and feelings.

One couple created the following fantasy regarding their bodily sensations. Tape this exercise so that you can experience it as you listen:

Your feet are on a soft cloud of white puffy cotton. They are resting on the soft, puffy cotton, being relaxed and soothed.

Your legs are on a soft cloud of white puffy cotton. They are resting on the soft puffy cotton, being relaxed and soothed.

Your body is on a soft cloud of white puffy cotton. It is resting on the soft puffy cotton, being relaxed and soothed.

Your arms are on a soft cloud of white puffy cotton. They are resting on the soft puffy cotton, being relaxed and soothed.

Your head is on a soft cloud of white puffy cotton. It is resting on the soft puffy cotton, being relaxed and soothed.

You are on a soft cloud of white puffy cotton. The cloud is floating through a blue sky. The warm yellow sun is shining on you. You are being relaxed and soothed.

They taped this exercise and both enjoyed it often. This was created as a response to question number 3.

Question number 18, "Imagine yourself performing a crazy sexual act," elicits a great many responses which are, of course, not crazy at all. Few things really are (see Chapter 20 for more about this) but many are really fun and exciting for couples:

"Let's make love in the car again, like we used to. . . ."

"I can see myself making love outside somewhere, like on a

beach or something where it's really dangerous, and we might be seen. . . ."

"Let's make love in the bathtub. . . ."

"I always wanted to have intercourse while I'm tied to the bed and making believe that I can't get up, and that I'm fighting with you as you thrust into me."

These remarks were made by shy, retiring people who found it very difficult to fantasize, to express their fantasies, and, even more, to act out their fantasies. Answering the questions is a first step to greater freedom. Being able to write down words which express your innermost desires somehow unlocks and releases you, makes you better able to express yourself. If you're lucky enough to have an accepting partner who is willing to fulfill your fantasies and enjoy them with you, you'll find even greater support.

I realize that these questions are not easy and that acting on them after responding to them is difficult. But I also know that you will benefit so much from the fun and excitement of being able to respond and to act that I urge you to make every effort to benefit fully from this questionnaire and from the next one.

The following questions are more specifically aimed toward increasing awareness of bodily responses to sexual fantasies. It is important that you learn about your levels of excitation. If you are working alone, please learn as much about yourself by responding to every question.

You may feel silly or embarrassed by some of the fantasies which come into your mind. You may even think them "crazy" or "kinky." You may have fears about expressing some of your thoughts. Please remember that communication is of the utmost importance. When you learn to share your fantasies, you'll find that most of them can be enjoyed together. Others can be laughed at or discarded, or enjoyed only in thought with each other. But share them—don't deprive yourself and your partner of what might be an unforgettable sexual experience. Being silly or kinky or crazy is wonderful. Remember how it was when you were a kid, rolling down hills and running into the wind? You're still entitled to be as wildly excited as you were then. Do it. Fantasy is a powerful tool which can help you toward these moments of gay abandon.

It is also a sensitive instrument which can be used to sexually stimulate, slowly and subtly, so that the excitation levels can be observed and even controlled. While making love, very often one partner's level of excitation is far above the other's. This works negatively, since there is pressure on the partner who is at the plateau stage and ready for orgasm while the other is still at the excitation stage. By using the fantasy that the slower partner prefers, this excitation level will be raised more quickly.

Complete the following questions so that you can become aware of what fantasies mean to you personally and how they can help you to raise your excitation levels to enjoy sex more fully. Answer these questions on your own at first. Discuss your answers with your partner—if you have one—after you have both completed the questions you have decided to answer. As with the first questionnaire, you may not wish to answer all of the questions. Please decide which ones you will each reply to before you begin. Do not speak to each other until you have answered all the questions you have agreed to answer. As with your other discussions, you may wish to tape this one and learn by listening to your remarks:

(1.) Have you ever had any sexual fantasies?

(2.) What do you fantasize about usually?

(3.) What actor/actress do you fantasize about, if any?

(4.) Would you share your fantasies with your partner?

(5.) Would you want your partner's permission before you would share your fantasies?

(6.) What do fantasies do for you when you have them?

(7.) Do you fantasize, or wish, that your partner would do something in particular? If so, what is it?

(8.) Would you be willing to fulfill the fantasies of your partner if they were in the realm of possibility? (Wear a black leather belt, eat whipped cream from his body, do a dance, etc.)

(9.) Do you want your partner to share his/her fantasies with you? Will you give him permission to do so?

(10.) What do you really wish for and/or dream of when you're making love?

(11.) Do you have fantasies of making love with your partner in new places, positions, or at different times of the day?

This questionnaire has been helpful to many people. Not only do they become aware of what excites their partners, but also of what excites them. They find that they can fulfill a lot of the fantasies and have a great deal of fun and pleasure doing it.

This is also helpful in avoiding boredom in the bedroom for couples who have been together a long time. I recommend that these two questionnaires be completed again . . . and again. Each time, your response will be different and may add excitement and pleasure to your sexual life.

An important factor in filling out these questionnaires is communication. I cannot stress enough how important it is to communicate with each other to the fullest extent possible. I do not advocate telling each other everything about everything. This is not only impossible, it is not even a good idea. I do strongly feel that the more you can share with each other about your needs, your desires and your hopes, the better chance you have of responding to and fulfilling each other's needs.

Open communication and honesty in the area of sex creates an atmosphere of trust and a bond between two people who are with and for each other. Working and caring for each other are most essential to the success of "Help Yourself Sex Therapy," as they are to the success of your life together and your happiness. If working alone, remember the more you learn about yourself using these techniques, the easier it will be for you to communicate when you are with a partner.

I've received hundreds of fantasies which were written by patients as a result of the questionnaires in this chapter. The following from Tom and Diane—a couple who successfully completed the program—is one of my favorites, so I share it with you.

This couple was creative and loved to use their talents in their lovemaking. They created images in each other's minds each night which were very elaborate and romantic and which turned them on. Here is one of their marvelous images:

"I (Tom) am walking into a large room. I notice there is a swimming pool in the middle of the room. The pool is not full of water, but it is full of whipped cream and in the pool are many, many women. They are all jumping up and down in the whipped cream, covered from head to toe. I don't recognize any of them, they are so covered. I get into the pool and begin eating my way through the pool. I am licking whipped cream from faces, from legs, from breasts, from stomachs. Suddenly, I notice that I am licking more whipped cream from one particular breast than from the others. I don't want to leave this particular woman for some reason. I begin licking the whipped cream from her other breast. I then reach up and wipe the cream from her face and look into the most beautiful eyes I have ever seen and at the most perfect nose and mouth. I bend to kiss the mouth of this marvelous, beautiful woman, and I say, "Diane, even in a pool of a hundred women, covered from head to toe with whipped cream, I can taste the deliciousness of you, and I choose you above them all."

This is a turn-on for several reasons. The image of many women, nude and covered with whipped cream, is in itself exciting to many people. But, for Diane, the excitement is knowing that Tom will find her and favor her above all. Also his use of imagery and his romantic language is very exciting to hear and certainly stimulating.

As you create the fantasies and images required of you by responding to the questionnaires, as you delve into yourself to become aware of what the answers to many of these questions are, you will be learning about yourself. Your secrets, your dreams, your wishes. You will be learning about how your body feels as you verbalize the secrets you've kept inside of you, and how you feel as your body responds to these thoughts and images.

You will learn the turn-ons, the turn-offs for yourself and for your partner. You will learn how to use your imagination, and how to increase your creativity and develop your own unique style and technique in lovemaking.

These questionnaires are designed to help you bring up, out of yourself, all of the knowledge and awareness which are already there, but lie dormant within you, untouched, unseen.

Knowing your body and how it responds to various stimuli, knowing your mind and how it responds to various stimuli are steps toward becoming a fuller, more complete person. By following the exercises in this chapter, you have taken those steps toward deeper knowledge, deeper awareness.

Continue to use the tools of imagination and communication you have just mastered. They are yours, and can be wonderfully exciting door-openers for you for the rest of your sexual lives. Remember, your mind is your most sensual organ.

CHAPTER 9

Sexual Sharing

THE art of sharing is a complex and difficult one to master. It calls for abilities and characteristics which far too many people lack. But if a couple is willing to speak with each other, tell each other what it is they want and how they want it, the art of sharing is already more than 90 percent learned.

I base this on what I have learned in years of working with couples. When sharing takes place, it is not a one-way street. One gives and the other takes, but the one who takes gives something else, and the one who gives becomes a taker as well. Sharing is not just giving, as so many people assume. It also involves the act of reciprocity.

A child who has a candy bar splits the bar in half and gives half to his friend. He GAVE, shared, his candy bar. The child who took RECEIVED half of a candy bar. So here we have the GIVER and the RECEIVER. But let's look at the scene a little more closely. The GIVER is smiling happily handing over half of his candy, because the RECEIVER is smiling too, saying thank you, showing that he is happy and appreciative. At this point, the GIVER and the RECEIVER are merged. They become one, each giving and taking, to and from each other. It is the richness of sharing.

Life is a series of sharings. Loving is a series of sharings. Sex is a series of sharings. Communication in its fullest and most rewarding sense is a constant series of sharings.

You have completed several exercises in the previous chapters. You have been involved in constant sharing, a constant giving and taking. Each time you revealed a hidden wish, opened up a part of yourself which had previously been withheld, spoke candidly and freely, you were involved in giving and taking.

You gave pieces of your innermost self, but in the giving you took too. You were heard and listened to and given sympathetic understanding and responses. This is giving and taking.

An example of this, more complex than the children with the candy bar but easy to understand, is the case of a couple who worked with do-it-yourself sex therapy and sent me their completed questionnaires, along with their remarks.

Cynthia and Joe hoped to add some spark to their sex life. They were especially interested in enhancing their sensuality and becoming more abandoned during their sexual activities. Completing the questionnaire in Chapter 8 was an important step for both of them toward their goal.

They discovered so many things about each other through their responses about fantasies and preferences that they were able to add excitement and joy to their love life to an even greater extent than they had hoped. The major reason for their success was their ability to share—to give and to take. A perfect example was given in Cynthia's response to the question: "Do you want your partner to share his/her fantasies with you? Will you give permission to do so?"

Cynthia's answer: "Yes, I do want to share and have you share with me. I not only give my permission, but I pray that you will share with me, because you're so much freer and more creative than me. You can add to my life if you will only stop worrying about hurting my feelings."

How is this the same as the two children with the candy bar? Cynthia gives the candy when she says: "You're so much freer and more creative than me." The compliment, the respect, the "looking up to" Joe are as delicious as any candy could be . . . more so. He revels in the good feeling she has about him, but mostly in the knowledge that he can now be free to express himself. In this freedom of expression, he will be giving her joy—a twofold pleasure, for this will give him joy too.

Please reread the last few paragraphs. I have followed this simple premise throughout my years as a sex therapist. I offer it to you and ask that you follow it, attempting to establish a system of communication, a system of giving and taking, with your partner. The following techniques are specifically designed to help you.

I have developed a questionnaire which I ask you to complete with the understanding that when you have both completed it and shared your responses with each other, you will begin to work. If you are working alone, you can use these skills to establish a relationship. You can even use them to get to know a stranger. I use the word WORK, because that is what you will be doing. The work is to begin the art of sharing with each other in order to fulfill your requests and needs and wishes without either of you taking too big a piece of the candy bar. Answer the questions honestly and without reservation. The compromising and sharing will be easier, if you are honest and direct:

INCREASING YOUR COMMUNICATION SKILLS
    (1.) I am very happy when you——.
    (2.) I am excited when you——.
    (3.) I am satisfied when you——.
    (4.) I am totally dependent on you for——.
    (5.) I really need you when——.
    (6.) It is important to me that you——.
    (7.) When I'm sad, I really wish that you——.
    (8.) When I'm angry I wish that you would——.
    (9.) Please do this one favor for me——.
    (10.) I can never, ever, ever again——.
    (11.) If you don't stop——I'll go mad.
    (12.) I especially like to give you——.
    (13.) I really like you when you——.
    (14.) Don't ever, ever, ever——.
    (15.) Please——.
    (16.) Aren't you ever going to——.
    (17.) There's one habit you have got to——.
    (18.) If only——.
    (19.) It hurts me when you——.
    (20.) The best thing you can do for me——.
    (21.) Loving you means——.
    (22.) How would you feel if I——.
    (23.) I always, always want you to——.

(24.) Give me——.
(25.) I deserve——.

This is a very difficult questionnaire to respond to. Please take your time, and please be sure to be totally honest and direct. Both of you must agree that you will discuss your answers with each other and begin the sharing process of giving to each other, so that both of you will be taking from each other as well.

Go over each of your responses, one by one. Agree on all of those which you can agree on easily and quickly. For example, one woman in response to number 6 wrote: "It is important to me that you tell me you love me at least once every day." Her partner immediately promised that he would, but he asked her to please remind him in some way, if he forgot. She was reluctant to do that, feeling it would take away from his sincerity. They then compromised by devising a subtle signal which she would give to him to remind him.

This compromise served several purposes. He got his way because he wanted her to realize that he did feel warm loving feelings, but that he "forgot" to say them or just didn't think about it. She got her way, because she did not have to verbalize and actually "ask." The signal form of "asking" was a face-saving device for her.

As soon as you have settled those questions which you can agree on easily, begin to discuss the other questions one by one. Don't try to resolve all of the requests and wishes immediately. Sometimes you will come up against some very difficult situations which can't be resolved.

One man responded to question number 11: "If you don't stop SMOKING, I'll go mad." You can easily see that his partner couldn't promise him immediately that she would stop smoking. But they did work out a compromise whereby she did not smoke in front of him unless she absolutely had to. They even decided what times she would "have to": when they had company in the house, and she couldn't excuse herself to go into another room, when they were in the car on long rides and she couldn't wait until they reached their destination and when they were at her mother's, because she didn't want her mother to know that they were having any conflict over her smoking.

You can see that each of these questions may take a great deal of time and effort to discuss, to come to some sort of resolution about and to "give and take" to each other so that each of you will be satisfied with the result.

If you come to an impasse, put the question aside and come back to it at another time. You may even wish to make a date with each other as to when to discuss the problem area. This is suggested, because it is always helpful to have a special time to discuss problems with each other.

I strongly believe that anyone who reads this book—anyone who is interested in growth—can use these communications skills to break through an impasse, if he has patience and faith in himself.

This brings us to a technique which has been very successful for all of the couples who stayed with it. I recommend that you decide, together, to follow this at a certain time each day, early in the morning when you first awake, or at night before retiring. It seems to work best with those couples who decide on a scheduled, consistent, ritualized time and place. Do this no less than once a day as long as the nondemand, nonsexual contract is in effect.

When you have made your decision, do the following:

(1.) Set an alarm clock for 10 minutes (no less than 5).
(2.) Sit down facing each other.
(3.) Place your hands on each other's knees.
(4.) Have your knees touching your partner's.

(Note: it is very important that you follow instructions exactly. Physical contact and eye contact encourage open and honest communication. They also discourage anger, loud shouting and breaking off discussion. Maintain your contact with each other for the full duration of this discussion period.)

(5.) Begin your discussion with whatever is on your minds at the time. It may be a topic you've previously decided on discussing or it may be something spontaneous. It may be a problem you haven't yet resolved. Begin the discussion.

(6.) Maintain your position and continue talking until the alarm goes off.

(7.) If there has been no resolution and an argument has ensued, the contract is that the conversation will END with the sound of the alarm. No further talk will be allowed.

(8.) If the conversation has been pleasant, everyday chatter, it also ends with no further discussion.

(9.) The sound of the alarm means the end of the discussion.

(10.) You must both adhere to this rule strictly.
(Note: otherwise, even if the conversation is peaceful, it may develop into an argument after the ritualized contact and ten-minute time schedule. Of course, you can extend the time period, but to no more than 20 minutes!)

Try to make this time as meaningful and productive as possible. Bring up troublesome topics, painful situations, gripes and criticisms. This is the time during which you both agree to respect each others feelings with as much understanding and acceptance as possible.

As you read about this technique, it may seem like an impossible task to you, or perhaps silly and worthless. I have heard remarks like these from couples to whom I've suggested it. But when you try these techniques and really take them seriously, you will discover for yourselves that they work.

They are practical and easy-to-follow, but in order for them to work for you, you must take the responsibility to do them. Don't just read about it. This book is designed not only to enhance your sex life but as an approach toward living together and communicating with each other in fuller, more expressive, more exciting ways.

CHAPTER 10

The Lovemaking Plan

HE looks at her, she looks at him . . . bells ring, lights flash, the sky lights up with miraculous color. They rush into each other's arms and explode in a frenzy of passion and love.

It sounds wonderful, doesn't it? But we know this doesn't happen very often—if at all. We certainly read about it, and have other people tell us what sex "should" be like, but we know that in real life, real people do not have this experience.

Working with many couples over the years, I have an indisputable fact: those who are willing to *work* at having good sex seem to have the most enjoyable and fulfilling sex life. They discuss sex with each other, they decide on what they like and how they like it, they play games during sex—role playing, fulfilling fantasies, exercising, teasing—in general, having fun with sex. They make *decisions* regarding the sex activity. This is contrary to popular romantic belief, but it is true: "good" sex is the result of hard work.

This chapter is intended to be used as a guide to lovemaking—to caring, to romance, to giving and to taking. You can personalize the ideas and suggestions any way you wish.

The lovemaking plan is not as essential as the *Nondemand, Nonsexual Contract,* and the *Let's Really Try Contract* that you are fulfilling. But the information you will learn about your own and your partner's responses will be infinitely beneficial to you in improving your lovemaking practices. If you are working alone, this chapter should help you discover what you'd like and how you'd like it. With this knowledge, you will be more likely to get what you want when you are with a partner.

Plan-making works. It lets you focus on what you want and

helps you to get it. In addition, many couples feel that, with a plan, they not only know what they want and can find ways to get it, but that planning commits them to fulfilling each other's needs.

At first, many couples feel there is a mechanical quality to these techniques and procedures. But this disappears as couples begin to benefit from the techniques described. In fact, they derive so much pleasure and gratification from the process, they feel more "human" and personally satisfied in their lovemaking than ever before:

Lani and Jim are lying on the bed facing each other. They are looking into each other's eyes, breathing very slowly and deeply. They are concentrating on their breathing, saying to themselves, "Air is coming in, air is going out," as they slowly begin to relax.

They begin to breathe in unison after a few moments, without even realizing they are doing so. It seems to come naturally after a while. They slowly begin touching each other's face, exploring lovingly and gently with their fingers. They lick and nibble each other's fingers as their lips are touched, continuing to look into each other's eyes and continuing to breathe in unison, keeping their minds "quiet," only their inner voices repeating: "Air is coming in, air is going out."

The room is dark except for a flickering candle; and silent except for the sound of Indian music, playing in the background, which both Lani and Jim love. They begin to explore each other's hands and arms. Their toes begin to touch and their feet and legs intertwine. They massage each other's legs with pressure and rubbings of their legs. They have an arm conversation, allowing their arms to dance together with the flickering of the candle reflected on the ceiling.

They watch the rhythmic movements of their shadows as they intertwine arms and hands. They allow the sound of the music to penetrate their bodies. They say to each other: "Let the music come into your body as it has come into mine. Let the rhythm come through your feet, up through your legs, stomach, shoulders, all the way up into your face." (They are using some of the image-making processes they have learned and now enjoy so much they use them often.)

Lani and Jim are following a lovemaking plan they devised together. They decided to use a relaxation technique each time they made love. They decided to have candlelight in the bedroom and music playing. They decided they liked rubbing each other's bodies, massaging, and playing with each other slowly and sensually. They decided they liked the image-exercise of allowing music to come into their bodies. They realized they both enjoyed speaking to each other during their lovemaking, relaxing each other and sharing feelings.

Lani and Jim love applying the various decisions they reached by completing the questions in this chapter. These questions will help you design a lovemaking plan too, which will not mechanize your lovemaking but enhance and energize it.

Sharon and Bob also enjoy the pleasures of making love as they want to, when they want to and in the environment they've planned. And they've found that having this plan, having made this commitment to each other and with each other, their lovemaking is more frequent and pleasurable:

The last of their four children is in bed, the house is straightened and for Sharon and Bob, it's finally "their time," as they call it.

They have found that stretching their bodies through exercise helps to relax and calm them after a long, tiring day. They have developed an exercise routine which they do together—touching their toes, bending from side to side, and backward, etc.

They take a shower together every night as part of their "contract." They wash each other and shampoo each other's hair. They dry each other and go to bed nude.

Up to this point, their nights have become ritualized, to the extent that they follow this procedure. They have also found that they love looking at each other for a while before falling asleep. At times, the looking turns into deep breathing together, into touching each other and very often they make love. There are other times when they fall asleep without any lovemaking, but with feelings of contentment and good feelings about each other.

Sharon and Bob were not dysfunctional when they came to me for treatment. They were bored with each other and usually "too tired" to make love. The plan which they devised has worked very well for them, the ultimate goal being that they do things together and pay attention—in a caring and loving way—to each other every single day of their lives. Being realistic about their situation and their time schedule, this is the system they have developed, and it works well for them. When they do make love, which is certainly much more often than before, they are both orgasmic. They are now very satisfied with each other and with their sex life together.

Lorraine and John also benefited a great deal from their lovemaking plan. They learned a great deal about each other, and were able to use this guide for personal benefit.

Lorraine and John began sex therapy because Lorraine was nonorgasmic. They were both concerned—John as much as his wife. After following help-yourself-sex-therapy for four weeks, Lorraine is now completely orgasmic and has reported multiple orgasms on several occasions.

In their own personalized guide to lovemaking, they decided there was one very important factor necessary for Lorraine. She needed a great deal of "being given to" before she could really feel loved and wanted. This is their style of lovemaking:

John has developed a sense of what gives Lorraine pleasure, and he makes the effort to bring her small, inexpensive gifts. Sometimes it is a flower he's picked from a neighborhood shrub, sometimes a poem he's written, but it is always a gift. He shows her as much attention as he can.

When they are alone, they both enjoy bathing each other and following this with a massage. They sleep nude every night now and often the massage is the beginning of an exciting and fulfilling sexual experience.

John feels that sometimes the effort he makes is contrived, but because he wants Lorraine to be happy, he is rewarded tenfold. Lorraine is so much happier now that her body experiences the delights of orgasm that she is more giving and appreciative of all of John's loving and caring gestures.

They are both very aware, at this point, of what gives each of them the greatest pleasure. During sex, they both give freely and without the inhibition and fear of failure of the past.

"We respect each other so much more now, we know our

needs and we love each other enough to want to fulfill these needs. Sex therapy, we love you." (From a letter written by John and Lorraine).

I am not suggesting that you must have a ritualized or regular pattern of lovemaking. I am merely relating to you the experiences of some of the many couples I have worked with. I have learned a great deal from these couples.

One of the most serious barriers to a good sex life together is boredom. All too often couples begin to take each other for granted. They become a habit to each other and boredom, the insidious enemy of vitality and life, begins its corrosive attack.

For this reason, I do encourage couples to plan ways and means by which to continue their lovemaking in as exciting and stimulating a way as they can.

Awareness that sex is not really the most natural act in the world, that pleasure not only can be stimulated and increased by various means, but should be, is important knowledge. But these needs are very personal and private. Only you can decide how you can best stimulate and increase your sexual pleasure.

I have developed an outline and questionnaire for this chapter which have proved helpful to many people in this regard. After you have mastered the techniques in Chapters 6 through 9 *and not before,* fill out the questionnaire. Again, I suggest that you each fill it out separately, then share your responses with the other. In this way you can decide on compromises and on taking turns with each other's ideas.

I know many couples who fill out this questionnaire once a month or so. They find they are constantly discovering new dimensions in their lovemaking desires, so that their patterns of lovemaking are always changing. This, of course, is highly desirable.

Also, whatever approach you decide on changes during implementation. For example, Lani and Jim like to begin making love by relaxing and concentrating on their breathing. At the same time, they are looking at each other. These looks, this "eye language," is spontaneous and unique each time. It is two loving, living, active human beings who are responding to each other's feelings at the moment.

I must point out that there is *no* contract—and I *never*

suggest that you make such a contract—which states that you
MUST make love. The contract stops at the point of practicing various arousal activities which both parties have agreed
to. Without feelings, lovemaking is empty and fruitless. By
contracting to relax each other, to care for and pleasure each
other, by touching and stimulating each other while nude,
couples usually have much more sexual activity than before
these behavioral changes.

Now, please complete the following questions. Make an
appointment to discuss your individual replies when you have
plenty of time so that you can decide carefully on your
lovemaking plan. Share your responses with each other honestly and fully and tape the discussion if you can:

(1.) WHEN?
    I would like to set aside the following times for "our times":
    At night from ——P.M. on.
    In the morning from——A.M. to——A.M.
    On Sunday afternoon from——to——.
    On Saturday night from——P.M. to——P.M. (A.M.)
    Other——.

Do not take this question lightly; it is essential. You must
plan your time together and make a contract to that effect.
One couple I worked with were both very involved with getting their doctorates. They would concentrate on their research so intently that they literally "forgot" about each other
until they were too exhausted to move. When they began sex
therapy, they agreed to set the alarm clock every evening at
10:30, and stop all work at that time. Wonderful results were
achieved with just this one simple step.

(2.) THE SETTING
    Of course, we all have fantasies but we have to be realistic
here, so when responding remain practical and keep your
requests within the realm of possibility.
    I would like to "be with you" on the (bed, rug, couch, car seat,
    other).
    I would like the room to be (dark, light, candlelit, other).

I would like the following music (type of music, name of record).

I would like the following scents (incense, spray of perfume, coffee, other).

I would like you to have (tactile stimuli such as velvet, satin or silk).

I would also like——.

(3.) RELAXATION

This area is extremely important. Unless the body is as relaxed as possible, free of tightness and tension, it is very difficult to achieve orgasm. All research indicates that the more relaxed and free you feel while making love, the more heightened and pleasurable your experiences will be. (Refer to Chapter 7 if you wish before responding.)

I would like to relax you by——.

I would like you to relax me by——.

Let's relax together by——.

My favorite breathing relaxation is——.

The following exercises make me feel good——.

(4.) BATHING AND SHOWERING

I prefer to (shower, take a bath, bubble bath, oil bath, other).
When you dry me please (rub lightly, rub hard, pat, wrap me in a towel, other).

(5.) IMAGE MAKING AND FANTASY

I would (would not) like to have pornographic literature——.

I would like you to tell me fantasies (read to me)——.

I would like to tell you fantasies (read to you)——.

I would like us to look together at pictures in the following magazines————.

I would like us to share our fantasies with each other (yes, no).

I get especially stimulated when you speak about——.

I want you to——.

You may not always want to use fantasy. For the times you do, have available literature and photographs of your own

choosing. Do use your knowledge of your partner's fantasies
to enhance your sexuality.

(6.) SENSUALITY
    I like these kinds of touching——.
    I like to be touched in these spots——.
    I like to touch you (where, how).
    I like to be touched with——.
    I like when you massage me (Explain how—hard, soft—where,
    with what—oil, powder, etc.)
Other likes (perfume you prefer, clothing or not, foods as
stimulants, etc.).

(7.) SEXUALITY
    My most sensitive sexual area is——.
    I like when you (describe the type of touch you like in this spot).
    I don't like (any activity which you don't want to engage in).
    I especially like (something you want to be sure is included
    regularly).
    I want to be free to (say certain things, do certain things,
    whatever you look forward to).
Other——.

After completing these questions and sharing your
thoughts and responses with each other, you are ready to
decide on your mutual approach to lovemaking. Don't forget
that these plans can be improved upon, changed often or
omitted completely. This is entirely up to you. If you decide to
make such a plan, it must be designed together and be very
personalized. Both of you must agree completely with all
phases of the contract if it is to work. Of course, this may
involve compromise, but the final form must be agreed on by
both of you. You can compromise—doing "her thing" one
week and "his thing" the next, changing often to satisfy the
desires of both of you.

When you have completed these questions, you will know
about your own preferences and your partner's.

You will know when you most prefer to make love. You will
know how you would like to arrange your environment—
using music, pillows, candlelight, scents, and so on. You will

know what types of relaxation exercises you prefer—which is so important. If the body is not relaxed, the mind is not quiet, truly pleasurable sex is not possible.

You will know if you like to bathe together, and how. You will know each other's fantasies. You will know if you want to be spoken to or not and how—"dirty" talk or love talk. You will know what you like to have touched and how you like to have it touched. You will know your special joys and pleasures and how to give them as well as how to get them.

Again, I am not saying that this plan is essential or that you should always use it. I know that it has proved beneficial to many. I share it with you and you must decide whether or not it's a tool you will find helpful.

The lovemaking plan is what *you* make of it.

CHAPTER 11

The Nonpenetration Contract

CONTRACT III

AT this point, you should have looked through the entire book at least once and then begun your program of help yourself therapy. You should have completed all of the questionnaires and exercises in Section II, Chapters 4 through 9. Your experiences have included relaxation exercises, sensual and sexual exercises, increasing your image-making and creative skills and a great deal of open and honest communication.

If you are working toward the amelioration of a sexual inability or dysfunction, you should now continue with the following two contracts. If you do not have an inability but are using *You Can Be Your Own Sex Therapist* to enhance your sexual life, then it is not necessary for you to complete the next two contracts.

Please remember that each time you have a lovemaking session, you are to repeat what you have been practicing these past days. Begin each session by relaxing each other, pleasuring each other and turning each other on in whatever ways you enjoy. Do not skip any of these experiences. They are essential to each lovemaking session.

You are now ready for CONTRACT III, THE NONPENETRATION CONTRACT. You will be involved with this Contract for approximately one or two weeks. As with the past techniques, do not go on to the next contract until you have completely mastered all of the sexual activities necessary for you.

If you are working alone, you will be building up your muscle control, becoming more and more aware of your body,

100

learning what excites and gives you sexual pleasure and, in general, to have a better sexual life. If you are with a partner at times, follow the procedures in this chapter being sure that you DO NOT penetrate until you have mastered full control of your sexual inability.

The *Nonpenetration Contract* is a statement agreed upon by both of you that you will engage in sexual activities *without penetration*. It is essential that penetration not be attempted until you are both fully aware that any inability you may be suffering is controlled to such a point that it is no longer an inability. The person desiring sexual improvement must be relieved of any pressure or demand for sexual performance. This need cannot be stressed too often. If a person has a sexual inability, fear of failure is infinitely more threatening and dangerous than the wildest, most fearsome adversary. No penetration means no possibility of failure, no demand to perform, no expectation. This is essential.

This contract is usually a simple contract for most couples to set up. However, I've been told by many that when sexual arousal becomes very intense, they attempt penetration. At that point, they experience a setback due to a feeling of failure. So please, please, use all of the methods to satisfy each other to the best of your abilities without penetration. Any sexual satisfaction is permissible—oral sex, manual stimulation, all types of foreplay and pleasuring—but NO PENETRATION is permitted.

Many couples specify in their contract the various methods they will be using to satisfy each other, including oral sex, masturbation, vibrators and turn-on literature both visual and auditory. But when you write your personal contract, be sure to include, above all, a full and complete commitment to each other that there will be no penetration, no request for penetration and no nonverbal hints for penetration—no possibility of penetration no matter what. If I'm repeating myself it's because I want you to realize the importance of this commitment.

This chapter and the following are specifically designed for persons who are suffering from a sexual dysfunction or inability. These contracts can also be used by persons who feel that they are not as sexually fulfilled as they would like to be and want to increase their physiological controls for an improved sexual life.

After completing Contract III in this chapter, you will then proceed to the chapter dealing with your particular dysfunction. The six sexual dysfunctions are dealt with specifically in Chapters 13 through 18.

Here are samples of Contract III as formulated by various couples:

A. "We agree to excite each other as we've been doing during the sensual exercises, using pornographic materials, massages, etc. We will proceed to oral sex or masturbation until we both climax. However, we will not have intercourse at this time."

B. "We will not indulge in sexual intercourse, but we will give each other sexual pleasure and bring each other to climax in whatever methods we care to and can think of besides penetration. . . ."

Please realize that a great deal of discussion and time should go into developing these contracts. You must be very careful about the words you use and the responsibility you take with them. Be sure you discuss them with each other to avoid any problem of semantics.

For example: What does oral sex mean to you? Does it mean both of you or one of you? Does it mean to effect a climax . . . with or without manual stimulation? Each word should be thoroughly discussed and agreed upon before the contract is signed.

During this phase of "Help Yourself Sex Therapy"—after you have agreed on Contract III—you are ready for the specific exercises and techniques designed for your particular inability. Remember, you should have looked through the entire book at least once, finished all of the exercises in Section II, and completed all of the requirements of your first two contracts. If all of this has been done, and your third contract completed, please go directly to the chapter in Section III which applies best to the inability which you wish to cure. Read the chapter carefully, then begin using all of the exercises described.

When you can successfully exercise the kind of control you need to cure your inability, then—*and only THEN*—are you

ready for CONTRACT IV, THE FULL SEXUALITY CON-
TRACT.

At this point, turn to Section III, and the chapter which
deals with your problem. When you have mastered the techniques—and yourself—go on to the next chapter (12) and Contract IV.

CHAPTER 12

The Full Sexual Activity Contract

YOU have completed all of the exercises in the chapter in Section III dealing with your particular inability. You have gained control of your dysfunction to the point where you feel confident of success in your "Help Yourself Sex Therapy" program.

If, for instance, you have been working on premature ejaculation, you are now able to control ejaculation for longer periods of time. You are now aware of the premonitory stage—the warning signal that you are about to ejaculate.

If you have been working on impotence, you are able to attain and maintain an erection. You are able to control your bulbocavernosus muscle and are aware of what turns you on and what keeps you turned on.

Those of you with the problem of retarded ejaculation have been able to ejaculate while in close contact with your partner.

If you are a frigid or nonorgasmic woman, you have experienced orgasm and have become aware of your excitation stages and what turns you on.

If you are working on the problem of vaginismus, you are now able to insert objects into your vagina and are able to lubricate naturally due to the excitation your body is experiencing. You are also able to enjoy the penetration of fingers and can experience orgasm with this type of stimulation.

Please be sure that you are at the stage described briefly above for each of these dysfunctions—and described more fully in the chapters dealing with each dysfunction.

If you are at this stage, if you have completed all of the

104

exercises and have the knowledge and control described, you are now ready for CONTRACT IV, THE FULL SEXUALITY CONTRACT.

This is the final contract and probably the most important one. This contract cannot be rushed. Timing is very important. Only you can judge whether or not you are ready for it. It is essential to this contract that you begin penetration AFTER you feel secure in the CONTROL of any dysfunction you have experienced.

Allow yourselves a "timing and withdrawal" clause, so that if penetration *has* been attempted too soon—or if you feel that you want to go more slowly—there will be no unpleasant repercussions. For example, a man whose problem has been impotence may complete all experiences successfully and still feel on penetration that he may lose his erection. He must KNOW that he is PERMITTED to withdraw and that his partner will masturbate him, or have oral sex with him, until he again feels that he *wants* to attempt penetration.

A woman with vaginismus may be very receptive to digital insertion or vibrators, or the other methods of stimulation described in Chapter 17. But upon penetration, she may tighten up slightly. She, too, must KNOW that she is PERMITTED to stop the penetration and return to other forms of sexual activity, such as oral or digital stimulation.

The person with a strong need for sexual improvement must have this "timing and withdrawal" so that he/she does not feel pressured. He/she must also know that there will be no punishment, in terms of the sexual activity ceasing or being postponed whether for a few seconds, minutes or hours. He/she must know that sexual activity will continue even if penetration stops. For this reason, Contract IV is required to include the agreement that penetration will be attempted slowly and gradually at the individual's own pace. Sexual activity will continue with or without penetration, and no judgment of performance will be made.

You must both realize that this is a gradual procedure which requires care and respect for each other at each step.

Here, as an example, is a contract made between a man who had trouble maintaining an erection and his partner:

"We agree to begin to have intercourse. I will be in total

control of penetration and will withdraw whenever I feel I want to, and I may begin penetrating again when I feel I want to. We both agree to this and that we will continue oral sex or masturbation if I do decide to withdraw."

An example of a contract between a man with retarded ejaculation problems and his lady:

"We agree to begin penetration and continue thrusting for as long as I wish to. If I do not climax during penetration, I agree withdrawal will take place and be followed by masturbation or oral sex. I agree to withdraw if Sue becomes uncomfortable with the penetration, and we will both continue stimulation until climax."

An example of a contract between a nonorgasmic woman and her partner:

"We agree to begin penetration and thrusting until Phil climaxes, but if I have not climaxed during penetration, Phil agrees to either masturbate me to climax, or I will masturbate myself to climax while in contact with Phil."

You will note in these sample contracts that the person with the *greatest need* for sexual improvement is in control of the sexual encounter, because he/she is best aware of the needs, capabilities and limitations he/she is experiencing due to the dysfunction.

You'll note that each contract includes the statement that sexual activity will continue regardless of whether penetration continues or not. This is essential and must be included. There must be no sense of punishment, or judgment, on the part of the non-dysfunctional partner. If sexual activity stops during a time of great excitation, during a time when an attempt is being made at a successful, complete sexual encounter, the results can be very damaging. You must be willing to accept that sexual activities are multiple and exciting and satisfying in many ways. Climax can be achieved in whatever ways are possible until it is finally achieved during penetration. Actually, a large percentage of women—perhaps 60 percent or more—do not climax during penetration. This is perfectly understandable, since we know that clitoral stimulation is necessary for orgasm.

Remember, even when the sexual problem is eased and you have a full range of choices in your sexual activities, you will certainly continue using all of the methods which you enjoyed and experienced orgasm with, not limiting yourselves merely to penetration.

Your contract should be drawn up during a quiet time together. It should be done when you are ready to begin this particular phase of "Help Yourself Sex Therapy." Contract IV should be agreed upon *when the partner with the sexual dysfunction feels secure and in control of his/her sexual situation.* This contract is arranged when he/she feels ready *and not until then.*

You may think these contracts are not important and may want to begin the exercises without them. This is NOT a good idea. Please benefit from the experience and mistakes reported by those who tested *You Can Be Your Own Sex Therapist* and worked with me to develop this program. You have the opportunity to avoid many of the pitfalls which befell us and which we learned to avoid so painfully.

Please follow the procedures conscientiously. Take yourselves seriously, and KNOW that your life will change. Your enjoyment of sex and loving will change and you, yourself, will change. Remember, everything asked of you in these pages has worked for others and will work for YOU. You can be in control. With the systematic techniques described in this book you can *learn* to be in control. It's your choice.

SECTION III

THE CURES:
SAMPLE CASE HISTORIES

INTRODUCTION

THERE is a wide range of ways to achieve sexual delight. Just because your route is different does not necessarily mean you have a problem, or a dysfunction, or are not as satisfied as another person who claims to have "better" sex than you.

"I want you to teach me how to have multiple orgasms . . ." "I can hold an erection only for ten minutes—there must be something wrong with me . . ." "I can only have intercourse once a night, can you cure me? . . ." "Listen, every time a woman tells me what she wants and how she wants it, I lose my erection. I'm afraid I'm impotent . . ."

These are direct quotes from people who have called me asking for help due to the "problems" they felt they had. Whenever such situations are presented to me, I become very angry and frustrated at the pressure tons of misinformation about sex and sexuality puts on thousands and thousands of people.

Women who feel that they are dysfunctional or have problems because they do not experience multiple orgasms are typical of the results of the pressure of sex propaganda in our society. Not all women have multiple orgasms, nor do all women want or need this experience. Often, women are enjoying their sex life until pressured by a friend or acquaintance to "get better," like the woman who wanted to be "taught" how to have multiple orgasms.

If you can have intercourse once a night and do not want it again, there is nothing wrong or terrible about that either. In fact, if you're enjoying sex once a night you are in a better sexual position than most of the people I know! But because you hear that a neighbor enjoys it three times a night, you immediately rush to a sex therapist and ask for help. This is ridiculous.

I want to emphasize here, as strongly as I possibly can, sex is a very personal and individual experience. There is no doubt that we all follow a certain set of physiological experiences, as described in Chapter 2. But these stages are experienced in different ways by different people. There is a wide range of sensations, feelings, experiences and reactions. The physiological manifestations of the excitation stage can go anywhere from a slightly moist vagina in some women to a soaking, dripping vagina in others. The excitation stage for men can be anywhere from a very, very firm and hard penis, to a penis which is erect but still has some loose skin and is not fully erect.

Such variations are infinite and are discussed in Chapters 13 through 18, dealing with sexual dysfunctions. It is important that you realize that just because one woman somewhere had twelve orgasms in a row, this does not mean that you can learn to have twelve orgasms in a row, or that you would even want to. Just because one man can maintain an erection for thirty-five minutes and enjoy it, does not mean that you should want to do the same thing. Perhaps being erect for ten minutes or twenty minutes or five minutes is what you enjoy most.

The fact that you may not require sexual activity frequently is not a sign of a dysfunction either. Intercourse once a night is as normal and fulfilling and as good and pleasurable for some people as having intercourse three times a night might be for others. There is no hard and fast rule.

You are the final judge and jury of your own sex life. You know if you are having fun and pleasure. You know if you are satisfied and feeling good. If you do not like women to tell you what to do and how to do it, if that turns you off, then that's where you're at. It doesn't mean you have a "problem." You can avoid this type of woman. Of course, I'd suggest you try improving your communication skills and try to get past this situation in a relationship, but it is certainly not a *sexual* problem if you are functioning well in other situations.

Don't allow magazine articles and books and the gossip of friends to interfere with your own awareness. Don't hide your head in the sand either, though. If you do have a problem, if sex is not as pleasurable as you would like it to be, then become as aware as you can of possible ways to resolve your problem.

Be true to yourself and your own awareness of yourself. "Goal-oriented sex" which is rampant throughout this country is depersonalizing the lovemaking act, making a mockery of the most tender and beautiful moment we can experience. Let's keep lovemaking what it is and should be.

If you don't experience an orgasm every time you make love, you do not necessarily have a dysfunction. The "Orgasm-or-Bust" Syndrome is a perfect example of goal-oriented depersonalized sex. Two people jump into bed, or fall on the floor, or climb into the back seat of a car and go at it: "Let's have an orgasm. Did you, did you, did you—no, no, wait, I didn't." This is not any form or type of lovemaking. This is a mechanistic doing to each other. Yes, orgasms are magnificent. But, there is much more to an orgasm than the mechanical act of *making* it happen.

I feel that sexual partners who are goal-oriented have no pleasure in the love itself, the relaxation, the sensuality, the giving and taking, the tenderness. They are only thinking of the final goal: orgasm. This in itself dilutes the experience. This is cold, depersonalized, and, in many ways, emotionally destructive.

I tell everyone I work with: Sex is loving. Every moment of the experience should be enjoyable and exciting. I am not saying that you have to be in love, or be with a partner you are in love with to fully enjoy sex. I am saying that you have to have loving feelings and tender feelings for your partner of the moment if you are to truly experience joyful sex. Masturbation is pleasurable when done with a self-loving, self-giving attitude.

Then there's the "Let's be better than the Joneses Syndrome." It's common cocktail-party chatter, in these free and easy years, to talk about how many orgasms you had last night, "darling," or how long he was able to keep "it up." After one such cocktail party, a 26-year-old male called me asking for an immediate appointment. A friend had told him he could have sex seven times a night, every night. Until then he had been happy with one orgasm which usually took place after an hour or so of lovemaking.

You and only you can decide about your sex life. We are all

UNIQUE. Our needs, our responses, our desires are all individual and special. Remember, you need only to look into yourself to know what is right for you.

There are dysfunctions and problems which do present serious problems, however. They are not merely the result of the pressures of society or unfounded fears. What is important is to find if you really *are* suffering from a dysfunction and, if so, to KNOW that you can be helped.

The following chapters deal with the six major dysfunctions and treatment for each of them. If, because of a dysfunction, you are unable to attain the emotional gratification and physical satisfaction which the sexual act should provide, one of these chapters is for you. If you are in doubt about whether or not you have a dysfunction, then the information supplied should help you to decide and clarify the problem.

You are ready to work on the program specifically designed for your dysfunction—if you have one—*after* you have completed all of the chapters in Section II and have formulated Contract III, *the Nonpenetration Contract.* If you are at this point, turn to the chapter which applies to you. Remember, success in this program depends on your commitment to yourself, on your serious intent to improve your sexual life and on your following the program as precisely as possible.

Also, please remember that sexual enjoyment is as individual as fingerprints. When you are feeling pleasure and joy in your sexual life, when you are satisfied with what you are feeling and experiencing, when you have completely relaxed and sated your bodily urges, then you have successfully completed "Help Yourself Sex Therapy." What THEY do is not relevant (whoever "THEY" may be). It is what YOU do that matters.

CHAPTER THIRTEEN

Premature Ejaculation

PREMATURE ejaculation is one of the most common of male sexual dysfunctions. So common, in fact, that there are many slang expressions describing such a man, in general belittling and undermining him.

This is very sad and unnecessary. No one need suffer from *any* sexual dysfunction. The number of patients who have benefited from sex therapy indicate that the techniques developed are phenomenally successful. By applying the information and procedures that follow you will experience success and satisfaction.

You are a premature ejaculator if you are unable to control the release of your semen. You ejaculate upon attainment of an erection or directly after penetration. You may be able to maintain an erection for a few seconds, or even a few minutes, but if you ejaculate before you care to you are a premature ejaculator. You may even be able to maintain an erection for five minutes, but if you ejaculate without the awareness, "I'm now going to ejaculate," or the desire, "I want now to ejaculate," you are also a premature ejaculator. If you ejaculate with a flaccid penis see the chapter on impotence.

In fact, any male who does not control the release of his semen as long as he wants to is a "premature ejaculator." Let me state here that I am not talking about men who want to be sexual Tarzans and thrust for hours. I am speaking about men who want enjoyment and pleasure from sex, but are not getting it because their ejaculations are premature. If you feel that you are a premature ejaculator, that you are not being pleasured sufficiently during lovemaking, you may be feeling inadequate or lacking in virility and depressed. You may even feel you are a failure as a "man."

I will not negate your feelings and say that you shouldn't have them. I will say, however, that the following pages are filled with invaluable information, which, if used properly, will rid you of the onus you have placed on yourself. The physical manifestation of premature ejaculation you experience is only temporary—unless you have some physical or deep psychological problem.

First, please answer these simple questions:

When you masturbate are you able to maintain your erection for longer periods of time than you can while having intercourse?

If you stop the motion of masturbation, will the ejaculation be prolonged?

Are there times, or certain positions in the sex act, during which you can prolong the ejaculation?

The answer to each of these questions should be yes. If it is not, I recommend that you have a medical examination before proceeding with this program. You want to be sure that there is no physical impairment causing premature ejaculation. Such a physiological problem is rare, but you do want to be sure.

The problem in premature ejaculation is usually a lack of awareness of the premonitory stage of lovemaking. (Fully described in the chapter on the physiology of sex.) During this stage the man can use various methods to control ejaculation. He may use muscle control as discussed in Chapter 3. He may think about something else, like baseball. He may pull out, stop thrusting, change his motion or speed, or change the position.

But the male who is not aware of this premonitory stage cannot use any of these methods. He has not even developed any of them because his awareness does not give him the message: "OK, now do something to stop the ejaculation." Men suffering from premature ejaculation have their first awareness at the "point of no return." By then the semen is already projected outward.

To correct this condition, then, the man must learn to become aware of this premonitory stage and then trained to control the ejaculation. This dysfunction is easily treated with "Help Yourself Sex Therapy." The exercises and techniques described in this chapter will guide any man working alone, or any couple working together to prolonged sexual pleasure.

Manny called me for an appointment, saying that life had become unbearable, sex was a nightmare and he and his wife, Florence, had gotten to the point where they ignored each other for weeks at a time.

When they came to me, they had been living together for over a year. Florence kept insisting that she was very happy about EVERYTHING. Nothing bothered her. Manny interrupted her to say that it had been his idea to make an appointment with me since it was *his* problem. He asked Florence to leave the room, which she did willingly.

As the door closed, Manny said, "You see? That's what I mean. Whatever I tell her to do, whatever I say, it's like the gospel. She'll never complain about anything. I'm here because I come in thirty seconds, and I'm sure it's not the greatest for Flo. She does have orgasms with other stimulation, but I want to be able to make love completely, like other people."

I asked him if he'd be willing to repeat everything he'd said in front of Flo. He agreed, and when she returned he told her what he felt. With difficulty he said: "Stop being so happy about everything. You've got to tell me the truth when you're not happy, or want something to be different. We have to be honest with each other."

I asked them if they'd be willing to try "Help Yourself Sex Therapy," and they agreed. That first meeting with them was an indication of their need to improve their communication, and so I stressed the importance of completing the Chapter on sexual sharing. It is extremely important that you really talk with each other and share with each other your feelings and wants.

Manny and Florence read through the program first, as I suggest to everyone. They then began to work together on the exercises in Chapters 6 through 9 and developed contracts I and II together.

At the same time, Manny began to work on the following exercises on his own. These involve learning to control the bulbocavernosus muscle—the "sex muscle" described in Chapter 3:

(1.) When you do not feel the need to urinate, go to the bathroom and allow a small amount of urine to pass. Pull back the urine. Don't allow any more urine to pass. Repeat this. Allow a small amount of urine to pass. Pull back. Don't allow any more urine to pass. Continue this until you have voided completely.

You don't really have to be taught this technique at all. We've all experienced "holding it in." Try it right now. Pull on your muscle as if you are "holding it in." Feel the tightness just behind your testicles as you pull back. You may find it helpful to squeeze your legs together, or to pull your stomach in at the same time.

This is a wonderful exercise since you will have immediate success. Every man I've worked with has been able to effect control of his urine in this way. Success, full control, is a phenomenal experience.

Dr. Barbara Hogan of the Cornell Medical Center Sex Clinic has also found this technique, which I developed, to be extremely beneficial in helping patients to understand the process of gaining control.

(2.) Repeat this same exercise when you DO have to urinate. (Remember, you first practiced it when you DID NOT have to urinate.) Let a few drops of urine pass. PULL BACK. Don't allow any more urine pass. PULL BACK. Don't allow any more urine to pass. Repeat. Allow a few drops of urine to pass. Pull back. Don't allow any more urine to pass. Continue this until you have voided completely. Repeat until you have control of this technique.

(3.) Again, following the procedure of increasing the difficulty of each task, wait until you have to urinate and feel that you have a very full bladder. Allow a few drops of urine to pass. Pull back. Don't allow any more urine to pass. Feel the tightness in the muscle. Feel the flow of urine as you pull back. Repeat. Allow a few drops of urine to pass. Pull back. Don't allow any more urine to pass. Repeat until you have voided completely.

Continue doing the exercise as often as you need to until you are in full control of this process. Remember that you are teaching yourself gradual control. At first you controlled your urine flow when your bladder was quite empty. You were in full control of this process before proceeding to the next step; learning to control your bladder when you received the signal to urinate. Again, you had full control of this step before proceeding to the next step. Finally, I asked you to exercise control of your urine flow when your bladder was very full.

Follow this exercise in the order given, one, two, three. It's as easy as one, two, three to gain full control of each of the exercises before proceeding to the next. This will take you several days. You have to wait for the proper moment when you have to urinate and when your bladder is very full. You must practice as often as you can. You have to become aware of the sensations experienced when using and strengthening this muscle. All of this takes time. Do not rush. Do not skip anything. Be sure that you are gaining control slowly but surely.

As mentioned, an essential awareness for you is knowing when you are experiencing the premonitory stage.

Manny reported that as he gained control of his sex muscle, he experienced various sexual responses. He attained an erection at times and was beginning to become aware of the sensation of swelling in the penis, hardening of the testicles and a general feeling of excitement throughout his body.

He had gained full control of the urination exercises and was to begin the masturbation exercises. Again, these exercises are done by the male alone, in private, not with a partner.

MASTURBATION EXERCISES:

(1.) Begin to masturbate slowly. Use slow strokes and allow enough time between each stroke so that you are really concentrating on the sensations you are experiencing. When you feel any swelling of your penis at all (any enlargement) stop masturbating.

(2.) Again, begin stroking until you feel an enlargement of your penis. This time, stroke for a slightly longer period of time. Do perhaps one or two strokes more before you stop.

(3.) Again, begin stroking. This time try to be aware of your testicles. Are they tightening? Are they rising as though going up into your body? Stop stroking as soon as you become aware of these sensations in your testicles and of the enlargement of your penis.

(4.) Repeat again, stroking until you become aware of these sensations. This time try to be aware of the swelling of the vein along the outside of your penis at the point where it becomes enlarged and, when your testicles tighten and begin to rise, stop stroking.

(5.) Repeat again. This time try to be aware of the flow of fluid within your penis in addition to the other sensations. Stop stroking. At this point you may have to add another exercise. Merely stopping the stroking may not be sufficient to stop ejaculation. Another way of stopping the ejaculation is to use

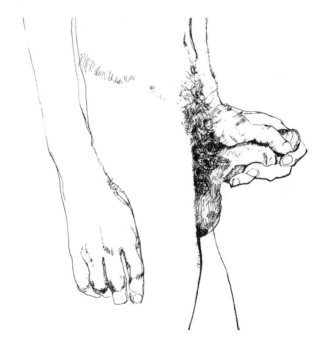

what I call the "thumb treatment." It is more commonly known as the "squeeze method." Using your thumb to exert pressure, push down very hard on the glans, the top of the vein running alongside the outside of your penis. This acts as a tourniquet— actually pushing the semen back down the seminal vesicle and preventing ejaculation.

Manny reported that he felt a swelling in his penis, a tightness in his testicles, a feeling that his testicles were rising and actually getting smaller and a feeling of pressure in his genital area. He was reporting all of the sensations involved in the premonitory stage. In becoming aware of this stage, he also became aware of when to stop stroking during masturbation. He learned when to apply the thumb pressure, if necessary, so that he could deter ejaculation. He was learning control. His problems with premature ejaculation were well on their way to becoming problems of the past.

As you become aware of these feelings, as you go through the exercises and gain control of the flow of semen, of your ejaculation, you, too, will be well on your way toward success.

These exercises will take you several days—perhaps a week or more. You will be doing them every day while you are also working with your partner, or alone, on the exercises in chapters six through nine. When you have successfully learned control through the urinary and masturbation exercises, you will be ready to transfer this control to working with your partner.

At this point, you should have completed chapters four through nine and executed Contracts I and II.

Manny and Florence had completed all of this—and Manny, working alone, had mastered the urinary and masturbation exercises—in about two weeks. They were now ready to formulate Contract III and begin some sexual exercises without penetration.

Contract III, the *Nonpenetration Contract*, read as follows for them: "I agree to masturbate Manny and to stop immediately when he tells me to, either by stopping completely any masturbatory movements or by placing my thumb on the glans of his penis in order to stop the seminal flow. I agree there will be no attempt at penetration whatsoever."

This is what they proceeded to do for the remainder of the third week of their therapy. Manny was very aware of his premonitory stage now and this awareness increased daily. He told Florence when to stop before he reached the point of no return while she was masturbating him. He was also able to control himself by pulling his muscle, so that he pulled the semen back. Together, they were controlling his premature ejaculation and reported feeling that their success was mutual and very gratifying. Their mutual goal of more control for Manny was achieved, and their excitement and pleasure with each other grew daily.

Most couples report that the male exercises a great deal of control during this time. Most often he does not need the woman to do anything other than stop masturbating as soon as he tells her to. The man is responsible for knowing WHEN TO STOP. It is his responsibility to tell his partner in time.

Florence became so tuned in to Manny's premonitory stage that she was aware of when to stop as soon as he was. She could feel his penis swelling, the vein filling up, the testicles hardening and becoming smaller as they rose. However, she waited for him to tell her when to stop, since it was important that he, not she, gain the control and the awareness.

They were, of course, still following the exercises in chapters six through nine, relaxing each other at the beginning of each lovemaking experience, using image-making and sensual experience to excite and pleasure each other and, in general, enjoying all of the pleasures they derived from these new techniques.

They were now ready for CONTRACT NUMBER IV— FULL SEXUALITY.

In the fourth week of their self-help program, they wrote Contract IV:

"We agree to begin intercourse by using only those positions in which Flo has good physical control, such as the female superior position. In this way, when I feel my premonitory stage or am about to come, I will tell Flo to pull off my penis, and, if necessary, use the 'squeeze method' at the same time to stop the ejaculation. When I am ready, Flo will resume the position and I will continue the penetration and thrusting. We may also use the side-to-side position, facing each other, or any other position we can think of in which Flo can control the pulling off and have the use of her hands quickly enough if I want her to use the 'squeeze method.' "

You will note that the side-to-side position is used because the female has greater mobility and can remove herself quickly from the penis. She can use her hand, if necessary, for the "thumb treatment." Also, men with this problem find it much easier to control ejaculation when they are in the female superior or the side-to-side position, since they are not actually doing all of the thrusting. The female is doing it as well or, in some cases, exclusively. (At the beginning of this stage of the treatment, many couples find it better if the male lies still while the female does all the thrusting).

Manny told me that he found it very helpful to verbalize to Florence during intercourse. He spoke of his feelings, his awareness, his various sensations: "I am now feeling my premonitory stage . . . the penis is swelling, the testicles rising, the testicles tightening, my stomach tightening, my breathing becoming more rapid."

Florence reported that she became very excited listening to him. Such verbalizations actually became a frequent part of their lovemaking. They both feel much freer now in talking about their feelings and desires during lovemaking.

The emotions you feel toward each other and toward yourself are essential in sex therapy. You must really want to have a more pleasurable sex life and be willing to work with each other.

This program can also work for men working alone without permanent sexual partners. A 42-year-old photographer was assigned to photograph me for a major newspaper. After taking my picture, he asked me what premature ejaculators can do to help themselves if they do not have a steady partner. I sent him the program and asked him to help test it. Three days after he began, he called to tell me: "You'll never believe this, but already I've learned control during masturbation."

He had spent several hours a day during the previous three days doing the exercises in chapters 6 through 9 and practicing the urinary and masturbatory exercises. He felt that he had gained a great deal of control, although he had worked extremely quickly. He said he'd spent about eleven hours

working on the exercises in chapters six through nine and about three hours on the urinary and masturbation techniques in the three days.

He called about a week later to tell me about a lovemaking experience with a woman he was dating. By using the squeeze method on himself as well as the muscle control exercises, he was able to effect control so that he was thrusting for three minutes. He used the face-to-face position, so that he could reach his penis with his thumb when he had to.

In my experience—and in the experience of the hundreds who have succeeded with *You Can Be Your Own Sex Therapist* —whether you are working alone or with a permanent partner, you can still use the described methods successfully.

You can develop your control to whatever extent you wish to, continually increasing the amount of time you maintain an erection before ejaculation. As you increase the amount of time you maintain an erection, please do not expect to jump from holding for one minute to holding for five minutes! It must be gradual. A good idea is to have one ejaculation, holding for a short time, and then attempting to hold for a longer time during a second penetration. Again, let me point out that being a marathon thruster is not the aim of good sex. Full pleasure and sensual excitement come with foreplay and tender and gentle lovemaking. So don't feel that it is imperative to thrust "forever."

Manny now calls himself a "marathon runner," since he can thrust for more time than he ever imagined he could. He has also found—as have many other men—that slow and gentle thrusting is very satisfying and can be maintained for longer periods than fast, hard thrusting. Most women enjoy this a great deal too.

Flo is not only orgasmic with clitoral stimulation, but is multiply orgasmic now because she does not have such direct clitoral stimulation. Previously, after an orgasm brought on by direct manual stimulation of her clitoris, Flo was so sensitive that she could not stand any continued contact with her clitoris. Now, with the more indirect stimulation to her clitoris achieved through vaginal penetration and thanks to the sensual exercises which are so exciting and such a turn-on to her, she is multiply orgasmic.

Manny's life has changed dramatically in other areas as well as in his sex life. He feels "taller," as he puts it. He has been promoted after working in the same company for seven years. His boss asked him where he had been all those years.

I saw Manny and Flo only once. All of their therapy took place at home, following the help yourself program. Manny and Flo were in on the beginning of *You Can Be Your Own Sex Therapist* and I thank them for their cooperation, as well as the cooperation of the many other couples who worked with me to achieve their own goals and to help me develop the help yourself approach.

From my experience with those who have followed help yourself therapy, I know you can succeed. Manny agrees. He just recently told me: "The fact that I did it myself was a great aid to my confidence. I didn't feel that I was leaning on a therapist and having to go to someone every week for 'help.' I think it was important that you gave me the material and told me to follow it on my own . . . at least for me. Thanks again."

It is true that your doing it yourself can serve as an added incentive and encouragement to your ego and sense of accomplishment.

One more thing I must point out here. Flo's way of dealing with Manny's problem before they came to me is too often typical. Many women living with men who suffer from premature ejaculation, or, some other sexual problem, are so worried about hurting their man's masculinity that they become totally passive and dependent. This does not help the man's ego. In fact, it damages it even more, because he is very aware that his partner is walking on "thin ice"—protecting his "problem" by avoiding it.

If you really want to help your man, join him in helping him help himself toward true pleasure for both of you.

CHAPTER 14

Impotence

"I need your help, I've been waiting for so long, and now I can get help."

There were tears in his eyes as he spoke. I didn't even know who he was, or how he had come to my office. He was sitting in the furthest corner of the reception room waiting for me. The secretary said he'd been waiting for two hours.

George was 54 years old two years ago when he first came for help. He was financially successful, a college graduate, content with his professional life, but he felt empty and incomplete as a man and as a person. He had never had sexual intercourse. He was never able to maintain an erection with a woman long enough to penetrate. He did climax when he was alone and masturbating, and he had been able to climax with oral sex and with masturbation with a female partner.

George was impotent. He had reached middle age and this problem had kept him from marrying, having children, and living the complete, fulfilling life he wanted.

Now he had met a woman who loved him and whom he loved. He did not want to burden her with his problem for the rest of their lives together. She was patient and understanding and very willing to come with him for help. As George said, "I don't want to lose this chance at really being alive with a woman I love."

Unable to see George and Betty because of an already crowded schedule, I suggested that they try the help yourself therapy program I was developing. They agreed.

George and Betty followed the procedure you have been following so far, but without many of the improvements and additions you are benefiting from.

Their Contract I, the *Nondemand Contract,* read as follows:

"I, Betty, agree that I will not, in any manner, either verbally or nonverbally expect, want, or ask for any type of sexual activity with George. We will both devote our time to learn the sensual and relaxation exercises and to experience each other as lovingly and warmly as possible. I will devote all of my energies towards the fulfillment of this contract."

They wrote Contract II, the *Let's Really Try Contract,* at the same time:

"We agree to help each other to learn all of the exercises described in Section II. We will share with each other as many of our feelings and thoughts as possible and truly try to follow the instructions closely and seriously. We have set aside two hours each evening so that we can work together. We feel very strongly that this is our primary and most essential interest at this time. Nothing will preclude our time for the therapy or our determination to succeed."

Betty and George realized that these contracts were essential. They knew that they should not be doing any of the exercises in this chapter—Chapter 14—unless they had followed the entire system up to this point. They were determined to succeed and followed each procedure very carefully.

Imagine the immense relief George felt when he signed the first two contracts with Betty. Having suffered from impotence and a sense of inadequacy for so long, he was now relieved of any fear of failure and shame. He was beginning a new journey of pleasurable physical activity which would not require any proof of sexual prowess of his part. He could not fail. He could only enjoy all of the experiences which were now "allowed" to him—the sensual, relaxation and image-making techniques.

The contracts helped Betty to become sensitive to George's deep sense of guilt and his desire to please her. She constantly reassured him, showing him that she was as excited as he was about the progress they were making. Besides a sense of gratification from helping George, she also felt deep pleasure in learning to be more sensual and to feel more relaxed with her own body and her own sensuality. The program was truly exciting for both of them.

As George and Betty followed the program in Chapters 5

through 9, they learned a great deal about each other. Their discoveries may be helpful to you:

Communication was vital. The more communication they developed, the greater their success was. Talking about how they would do the exercises, when they would do them, what the exercises meant to both of them, what problems they faced and what was pleasing was all very important. They did not merely begin to do the exercises. They needed the structure and control built into the program which I am constantly urging you to follow.

They discovered that pornography, turn-on literature, pictures and records and fantasies excited them a great deal. They followed my suggestions to use all of this material. They said later that if they hadn't "tried these novel ideas, they would never have known some of their most enjoyable sexual adventures."

In addition, Betty was relieved of the pressure of having to excite George. By reading turn-on literature to him and by looking at provocative pictures with him, she did not feel directly responsible for his attaining—or not attaining—an erection. She did not feel threatened. The words she read to him and the pictures she showed were a depersonalized method of stimulating him. After he was able to become excited in this way, Betty grew increasingly secure. She began to invent her own techniques, together with George, using turn-on literature at times but not always.

They followed the experiences in Section II for almost three weeks, working daily as they had promised themselves. They executed Contract III, *the Nonpenetration Contract,* before beginning the exercises in this chapter (as you should have), writing the following:

"We agree to engage in any sort of sexual activity which we prefer, or choose, at the moment other than penetration. We agree to pleasure each other in whatever ways we request of each other and to share with each other our feelings and thoughts regarding the experiences we indulge in."

By this time, George and Betty were closer than ever before and determined to succeed. They were working on "their problem"—not George's problem. This attitude freed George of embarrassment and inhibitions. Betty was very supportive

and loving throughout the therapy. Both evidently enjoyed all of the activities very much—as evidenced by the tape recordings they made.

Both George and Betty had orgasms during this phase of their therapy, the fourth week since they had begun the program. They masturbated each other, performed fellatio and cunnilingus and excited each other in all of the ways they had learned about. They continued sharing with each other in their communication exercises. They both loved to be massaged and still find this to be deeply stimulating and exciting.

Betty told me during a telephone call: "There's nothing like a massage for George's penis. He responds to it like an elevator responds to someone ringing for it to come up to the top floor. We both love it."

When George and Betty felt they were ready, they formulated Contract IV, *the Full Sexuality Contract* which George wrote:

"We both agree that during the lovemaking experiences we have this week, I will begin to penetrate. I will do this slowly and gradually. I will penetrate at the point of ejaculation for the first two times, after some masturbation. I will partially insert my penis at first and will also attempt some thrusting if I wish. If I feel a loss of my erection, I will pull out, and we will continue the sexual activity by masturbating. This will be the procedure until complete penetration is achieved and ejaculation is achieved during thrusting. Regardless of how many attempts are made, how often I have to pull out and continue other sexual activities, we will continue."

You'll notice the "escape clause" George wrote into the contract, as recommended. He could pull out without any punishment or discontinuance of the sexual activity. They both agreed that Betty would continue masturbating until climax if the penetration didn't succeed.

This is essential. The impotent man must not feel pressured; no sexual demands should be made of him. He must not feel that he will be punished or humiliated if he fails. There must be an atmosphere of freedom and pleasure without having any performance levels placed for him. The female, however, is also entitled to pleasure, therefore Betty was to masturbate, or be masturbated, until she climaxed as well.

You'll also note in the above contract that George states that he will masturbate before penetrating. This was his decision, because he feared that he would not be able to maintain the erection after he first penetrated. He was afraid that he would lose his erection too soon and would be unable to achieve ejaculation. He felt that he was "building in" further possibility of success by coming as close to ejaculation as possible before he penetrated. This is up to the patient. It does not work for some people, but it does for others. If thrusting is a problem and may cause the man to lose his erection, then this "escape clause" may be a good technique.

It worked very well for George. Since he knew that Betty was willing to continue sexual activity, regardless of whether thrusting and penetration succeeded, he did not feel pressured. This nondemand helped him greatly during his early penetration attempts. After three such attempts at penetration, George was able to thrust to ejaculation, thrusting for three minutes at the most.

I spoke to George and Betty recently. It's over a year since they completed this sex therapy program. They are both very happy together. George has been promoted twice in his job, and Betty claims to look ten years younger. Their sexual activity has increased, their "pleasure always rising," as Betty said.

George told me that he can attain erection during all of their lovemaking and maintain an erection long enough to give both of them pleasure. They still continue all of the foreplay, using the relaxation exercises, the sensual techniques which they've "learned to love."

I would like to share with those of you who are working alone the program Tim followed. I feel this can be helpful to you:

When Tim first asked me for help, I explained that many sex therapists feel that it is not practical to offer sex therapy to a person who does not have a permanent sexual partner. I told him that I had found that persons without partners had succeeded with the help yourself program. He agreed to work on his own, saying, "Without improving my sex life, I won't be able to get a woman. Women want good sex today. If they don't get it with me, they'll look for someone else, so I'll try anything."

He was feeling very pressured, very much in need of help, and was willing to work hard to cure his dysfunction. Tim was 45, divorced. He had felt inadequate, sexually, toward the end of his marriage. His wife had constantly belittled his poor sexual performance. He was suffering from financial difficulties, too, and she'd taunt him with: "The less money you have, the smaller your cock gets."

His teen-aged children often heard these remarks. Humiliated and enraged, he'd get more and more anxious in his desperation to improve sexually. His wife belittled him more and more. He could not achieve an erection during the last four years of his marriage with his wife or with any other woman. He was impotent.

After his divorce, Tim was afraid to attempt sex with any women for fear of failure. He labeled himself as impotent and felt he would always remain that way.

Tim completed this program successfully, proving that it can be the answer for you even if you are working alone. It is interesting that Tim's success may have been due particularly to the fact that he *was* working alone. He had such fear of failure with a woman that sharing the therapy experience with a partner might have proved too threatening for him.

He drew up the first two contracts with himself, making a commitment to himself that he would really work and detailing when he would work and how:

"I will spend one hour every evening following every exercise which it is possible for me to do alone. I will tape-record all of my reactions and all of the exercises, so that I can repeat them over and over to get the best out of them and to learn from them. I am doing this for me."

Tim developed his sensuality taking oil baths, bubble baths, massaging himself as completely as possible, looking at himself in the mirror as he touched and examined himself, touching himself with a variety of textures, smelling various scents —in short, following the suggestions in Chapters 6 through 9.

He learned to relax, to increase his image-making skills, to turn himself on with turn-on literature, with fantasy, with certain types of touching. He learned to pleasure himself as much as possible.

Tim discovered that by touching his own nipples he became very excited and attained an erection. Touching his anus and testicles also aroused him and helped him to maintain an erection.

Tim developed his muscle control fully as described in the chapter, *Put Power in Your "Sex Muscles,"* and in the chapter on premature ejaculation. With this muscular control he was able to maintain an erection. He taught himself how to move his penis from side to side and toward and away from his body in less than three weeks of practicing muscle control.

He then masturbated to the point of orgasm until he was able to control ejaculation using all of the methods he'd mastered. Tim now felt he was able to exercise a great deal of control. He was feeling very confident before he attempted any sexual contact with a woman.

Tim did not reveal any of this to the woman he made love with after he regained his confidence. The first three times he was with her, he used all of the techniques he'd learned in chapters six through nine. He even played some of the tape-recorded exercises for her, saying they were tapes he'd made from various books on yoga. He massaged her, bathed her, and pleasured her in all of the ways he'd learned to pleasure himself by following this program. Naturally, she reciprocated. Their first three lovemaking sessions were very sensual. She was very aroused. Tim did stimulate her to orgasm, but following the program religiously, he did not attempt any penetration or climax for himself.

His partner loved the experience. She said she'd never had so much loving attention. After the first three sessions, during which Tim did attain and maintain an erection, he attempted some of the sexual experiences described in Chapter 11, on the nonpenetration contract. Tim wrote the following Contract III for himself:

"I will not attempt any penetration regardless of what happens. I will have oral sex and will use masturbation while with a partner."

When taping his reactions to his lovemaking after he'd

formulated Contract III, Tim said: "I really think I could have made it, but I didn't want to push myself too much. I figured I'd better go slow."

He practiced all of the sexual activities other than penetration during the next two evenings he spent with a woman. He then felt ready for Contract IV, *the Full Sexuality Contract:*

"I will begin to attempt penetration. I will excite my partner a great deal first, because this excites me as well. I will use all of the techniques I know to make this successful. If I have to pull out, I will continue other sexual activity with her and not become discouraged and stop."

The next time he was with a woman, Tim followed all of the usual lovemaking techniques—massaging, relaxing, turning each other on and pleasuring in every way. Then, while engaging in oral sex and after attaining a full erection, he positioned himself so that his partner was astride him. In this position, he began penetration. He was able to keep his own hand at the base of his penis, continuing to stimulate himself: His partner liked this, too, because he was touching her clitoris at the same time. Although Tim was successful in this first penetration, he would have withdrawn if he'd wanted to, asking his partner to masturbate him or masturbating himself, as he had contracted to do.

Tim is no longer sexually dysfunctional. He continues using all of the exercises and techniques which he has mastered: "Not because I have to, but because I enjoy them. Women get so turned on by my relaxation tapes and the sensual stuff I do with them, I don't tell them anything. I just do it and they love it. Oh, yeah, so do I."

As Tim said, he doesn't tell his partners anything. Not one of the women he's been with since he began help yourself therapy has been aware of his "problem." He decided that he'd rather not share it and found that he didn't have to.

Tim is one of the men who worked alone in this program and succeeded. If you are working alone, you can succeed too.

You are reading this particular chapter because you have decided your problem is impotence. But, before you continue, let's be sure this *is* your problem:

If you have been unable to attain an erection from time to time due to fatigue, too much drinking, emotional stress, or

some other situational or temporary problem, you are NOT impotent.

If you are unable to attain an erection a good deal of the time; if you can attain an erection but lose it almost immediately; if you have not been able to culminate intercourse at all, then you are impotent.

If you can attain an erection during masturbation or at other times, then you do not have a physiological problem; but if you cannot attain an erection at all, you may have a physiological problem and should go for a complete physical checkup. Be sure that you tell your doctor why you want a complete examination, so that he makes use of all the necessary tests to discover if there is a physiological dysfunction.

If you feel at times that you are inadequate and would like to learn to maintain an erection for longer periods of time, then you can benefit from the following exercises too. They will help you to gain more pleasure from sexual activity more often, attain erections for longer periods of time and, in general, be more in control of your sexual life. But be aware that impotence exists occasionally in almost every man and can be a frequent, unwanted visitor in others who are not basically impotent but may be under undue stress.

Also, be aware that as you get older you will not be able to attain erection as often, or as quickly, as you did when you were young. Don't label yourself impotent because your body needs more rest between erections.

If impotence is truly your problem, continue with the following program:

First, read Chapter 13, the chapter on premature ejaculation. The exercises in that chapter are designed for the cure of impotence as well as premature ejaculation.

After you have written Contract III, you will add a prescribed set of sexual activities to your lovemaking sessions with your partner. You will, of course, continue the relaxation and image-making exercises, as well as the muscular control exercises and the turn-on methods.

Here are the activities you will include in sessions with your partner: Instead of masturbating yourself to climax in privacy and practicing control, you will begin to masturbate with your partner as soon as you can attain an erection. You will ask that she help you to practice control. You can masturbate yourself while she is in contact with you, or she can masturbate you. It is important that you attempt control of your ejaculation and maintain the erection for as long as you care to.

You can now have oral sex as well, maintaining your erection and controlling the ejaculation as you've been doing during masturbation. Again, use the most helpful of the controlling devices you've learned. Or, if you find it best, use all of them—the "thumb treatment," or total withdrawal from stimulation, muscular control, thought control . . . all of them.

You will be stimulating and satisfying your partner, bringing her to climax, using whatever methods you choose to excluding PENETRATION.

This stage is actually a practice stage. *You must stay in this stage of your therapy until you yourself are confident about your control.*

Ask yourself these questions:

(1.) Can I attain an erection?
(2.) Can I maintain my erection for a long enough period to experience pleasure for myself and my partner?
(3.) Have I really mastered the controls I need to attain and maintain an erection?
(4.) Am I satisfied with my progress?
(5.) Am I willing to begin penetration?

If the answer to all of these questions is yes, then you are ready for Contract IV, *the Full Sexuality Contract.* The next step in your therapy is to formulate this contract.

Most persons have been working at least three to four weeks up to this point, but schedules vary greatly so don't be concerned if you are taking longer than others. Don't rush. Don't skip anything. Guarantee success for yourself by following the procedures religiously.

Be honest with yourself when replying to the above questions. If you want to wait a while longer and utilize all of the experiences you've had for the past few weeks to become more confident and more proficient in your control, then do so. Be good to yourself. Don't enter Contract IV until you are SURE. This is the most difficult phase of the therapy. Take your time and be sure.

If you are sure, please return now to Chapter 12 and follow the instructions as you formulate the fourth contract. Here are the steps to follow *after* the contract is decided on:

Begin penetration when you are fully erect, having used excitation techniques, relaxation techniques and after you have experienced a great deal of pleasuring. *Do not attempt penetration unless you have been loving for a while and are very excited.*

Have complete control of when to penetrate, in what position to penetrate, and when to withdraw. Your partner must agree that you will retain complete control of these factors.

Stay as relaxed as possible. Utilize your awarenesses and your knowledge. Exercise your muscular control and all of the techniques you have mastered. Remember, this is a slow process. You have control. Your penetration can cease at any time you wish. Continue with other sexual activities, if you do decide to withdraw.

If you have difficulty attaining or maintaining an erection during one of your lovemaking sessions, you may want to attempt what is known as "stuffing." It is possible to penetrate the vagina with a flaccid—non-erect—penis. Many men become excited and attain an erection after the penis is within the vagina. This is because they are stimulated by the moisture and the warmth and the general excitement involved in penetration.

If you attempt "stuffing," be sure that your partner is sufficiently excited and well-lubricated, so that she will not experience any discomfort and so you will be able to penetrate more easily.

This holds true for any attempt at penetration on your part. Always be sure your partner is at the height of excitement and well-lubricated before you attempt penetration with either an erect or a flaccid penis. The more lubricated your partner is, the easier it will be for you to penetrate.

The female can help insert a flaccid penis if she wants to. She is more aware of where to insert the penis and how to

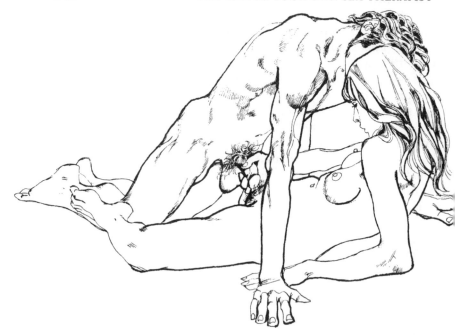

avoid any awkwardness and pain. At the same time, she can stimulate the penis to aid in attaining an erection as she inserts it.

In addition to "stuffing," there is another technique. This is remaining very "quiet and still" while in the vagina. It is not necessary to thrust or even move in any way. Just remain quiet. This is exciting and can help you to maintain or attain an erection. Merely enjoy the feelings aroused during penetration, the proximity of your bodies, and the kissing and stroking of each other as you maintain a "quiet" penis. Use muscular control at this time and experience your penis as it responds to the controls you have learned.

This phase of your therapy will take about a week or more. You will want to increase the amount of time you can retain an erection, build up your confidence with more and more successful penetrations and, subsequently, more frequent and longer periods of thrusting.

The length of time you want to remain erect, the amount of thrusting you wish to do is entirely up to you and to your partner. Lovemaking is an individual and highly personal experience. Only you can decide when you've reached a satis-factory stage in your lovemaking skills. Many persons continue to learn, to build their skills and controls and to be constantly creative and original in their lovemaking. Only you can decide when your sex therapy satisfies your own needs and desires.

Remember, remaining erect for long periods of time, strong thrusting and prolonged periods of penetration are NOT the essence of making love. As you discovered in your experience of sensuality and pleasuring, there is much more to giving love and joy to someone else, to feeling the loving warmth and beauty of a sexual relationship.

When you feel that you have successfully completed the therapy, answer the following questions:

(1.) Can I attain an erection?

(2.) Can I maintain my erection long enough to experience pleasure?

(3.) Have I really mastered the controls I need to attain and maintain an erection?

(4.) Am I satisfied with my progress?

(5.) Am I able to penetrate for sufficient periods of time to satisfy myself and my partner?

(6.) Am I able to thrust for sufficient periods of time to satisfy myself and my partner?

(7.) Do I want to continue to master my controls more efficiently for added pleasure?

(8.) Am I no longer an impotent man?

If the answer to all of these questions is a resounding YES, then you are another of the hundreds of men who have successfully completed *You Can Be Your Own Sex Therapist.*

But even now, please continue using all that you've learned. Don't let your lovemaking become run-of-the-mill. Now that you have mastered the body basics, you can go on to make your lovemaking ecstasy.

CHAPTER 15

Retarded Ejaculation

IF you suffer from retarded ejaculation, you are unable to ejaculate WHEN YOU WANT TO. This inability manifests itself during intercourse or oral sex. Despite the intensity of the thrusting, or the amount of time spent penetrating or having oral sex, you do not ejaculate when you are ready to.

You are, however, able to ejaculate when you want to during masturbation, especially if you masturbate when no woman is present. If you cannot ejaculate when you want to while masturbating alone, then you should consult a medical doctor to be sure that you have no physiological problem.

To some persons, this may sound like a marvelous "affliction," retaining an erection "forever," but those of you who have this dysfunction know that it is not marvelous at all. It is not even pleasurable. In fact, there is often pain associated with the inability to "let go." The emotions aroused are as negative and destructive as those occurring with any other dysfunction.

It is very important that you understand exactly what is happening with this dysfunction. All too often, the female feels responsible for her mate's not being able to climax. She feels she is not "sexy" enough, or a good enough sex partner. She may even feel a failure as a woman.

Too often, the male actually does blame his partner, feeling that she should be able to make him climax. He places the responsibility for his inability on her, and this is very damaging.

It is crucial that you understand from the beginning that there is NO blame, NO fault, NO responsibility. If you have a sexual dysfunction, YOU have it. If you have a partner, then you have the dysfunction TOGETHER.

Your partner is responsible to BOTH OF YOU to help you both achieve your common goal of a better sexual life. She is not the cause or the blame for your inability to climax with her, nor are you to blame for it. But you are both responsible for shedding it—if you want to.

As you experienced in the exercises in Chapters 6 through 9, it is possible to gain control of various sensations and have a great deal of pleasure with your new awareness. It is also true that you will enjoy new pleasures as you conquer your sexual inability. Through a variety of techniques described in this chapter, you will be able to acquire the ability to ejaculate when you want to, whether during penetration, oral sex, or while your partner is masturbating you—as you prefer.

You must accept the important facts about blame and cooperation fully and understand them before the actual treatment begins. This understanding is important for all couples whatever the dysfunction they are working on. Both parties must be with and for each other, helping and loving and caring in all of these treatment processes, or the chance for success is lessened.

One woman put it beautifully when asked if she would be willing to "do something for her man." She said, "Are you kidding? Do something for my man? We're doing it for *us.* That's why we're here. Sex is not a one-way street. We both need each other and want each other. So whatever it is, *we'll* do it."

Her partner looked at her with as much love and tenderness as I've ever seen on anyone's face and reached out to take her hand. These are the moments of beauty I see daily, moments which you, too, can experience by following the exercises and learning to communicate with each other as fully as possible.

All too often a sexual problem gets in the way of a couple's love and pleasure and corrodes the relationship. This was the case with Marty and Teresa.

They had been married almost three years. For seven months before calling me, they had not had any sexual contact at all.

Marty was suffering from retarded ejaculation. They agreed to practice "Help Yourself Sex Therapy" for several reasons. Their financial situation was such that any therapy charge was beyond their means. They could not leave their two children long enough to attend sessions, and they lived a great distance from my office and from any other sex therapist I could recommend to them.

Before the last seven celibate months, they had had intercourse less and less frequently. When they first started having sex together, Marty "pretended" to ejaculate after one hour, or longer, of actual penetration and thrusting. Teresa never knew. She was thrilled with their sex life. She felt that Marty was the strongest, most incredible lover she had ever known. (Not all women like to have sexual intercourse for such long periods; this is a matter of personal preference.) She was multiply orgasmic and enjoyed the intense stimulation.

Marty would often have pain from the buildup of pressure and pretended to climax when it became excruciating, or when he sensed that Teresa was tiring. He would pull out quickly and run into the bathroom where he would masturbate to climax, pretending he was washing or voiding. Marty couldn't understand what was going on. He said that often all he would need was two or three strokes of his own hand and the release would be complete.

Teresa was bewildered when Marty began losing interest in sex, because to her their sex life was wonderful. After ten months or so of their marriage, she did notice that Marty was still erect after he said he'd climaxed. When she remarked on this, he brushed it aside.

Teresa believed that Marty had gained another erection because he was passionate and wanted more. It was difficult for her to understand this man who had seemed to want her so much and who suddenly lost interest, or seemed to.

She felt rejected and hurt. He, on the other hand, felt that she was somehow to blame for his problem and so he deprived her of sex more and more.

"If I couldn't have it, why should she?" Marty told me. "But I didn't consciously realize at the time what I was doing. I was just losing interest and withdrawing from the discomfort of sex."

They began their treatment, as you have, by formulating Contracts I and II, the *Nondemand Contract* and the *Let's Really Try Contract*, according to Chapter 5, and by mastering the techniques in Chapters 6 through 9.

They experienzed no problems with this part of the treatment. In fact, they enjoyed it a great deal. They spent four weeks experiencing all of the exercises in these chapters. This is a longer time than most other couples spend on these techniques, but they had been celibate for seven months and were getting to know each other physically, intimately, as though they had just met. Also, they were very careful not to hit any snags, not to confront any possibility of failure. To make sure they took their time.

They were ready for the third contract after four weeks of working at least 45 minutes a day, a minimum of four days a week. Their third contract, *the Nonpenetration Contract*, read as follows:

"We agree to begin sexual activity by masturbating each other and having oral sex. Whenever Marty desires to climax, he will masturbate himself if he wants to. There will be no attempt to penetrate at all."

Marty and Teresa found, as do many couples where the male suffers from retarded ejaculation, that Marty could not ejaculate in Teresa's presence. While each of you will have to follow the procedures suggested according to your own needs, I present this case history because Marty had a most difficult problem. The program he followed is as detailed as anyone should require. (This is true, only if you are not deeply psychologically disturbed; in that case you require additional professional help.)

With retarded ejaculation, an additional technique besides the relaxation, image-making, fantasizing, and muscle-building exercises is employed. It is known as "desensitization." The male must desensitize himself to the problem of not being able to ejaculate with a female present. He must, therefore, ejaculate first at some distance from his partner, ejaculating progressively closer and closer to her until they are actually touching each other as he climaxes.

For his desensitization treatment, Marty masturbated in the bathroom with the door open while Teresa was in another room. He had some difficulty climaxing, because he was aware that Teresa knew what he was doing; but after two such attempts, he succeeded. On the second attempt, Teresa read some turn-on literature to him just before he began to masturbate. Marty feels this helped a great deal.

He then masturbated in the bathroom while Teresa sat in the bathtub with the shower curtain closed. Again she read turn-on literature to him. She continued reading all the time he masturbated until he climaxed.

Marty immediately got into the tub with her and they bathed each other. Marty said that this loving and caring directly after masturbating to climax was a wonderful experience. It helped him to realize that Teresa truly accepted what he was doing and loved him without having any bad feelings about it.

It was important that Teresa maintain loving and warm feelings toward Marty throughout this period. She did not judge him, or make any demands on him.

Marty was eventually able to climax while Teresa watched him masturbate. Again, they made love for a while first. When Marty was ready and wanting to climax, he got out of the tub and Teresa read turn-on literature to him while he masturbated. She also stood next to him, stroking his body and kissing him as he masturbated.

He was then ready to climax while making love, touching each other, having oral sex, stimulating each other in all the sexual ways they enjoyed. When he wanted to climax, he began masturbating, remaining next to Teresa but not really in direct physical contact with her. She continued stroking him and kissing parts of his body, maintaining some contact with him as he climaxed.

They were coming closer and closer to their goal of penetration and climaxing during penetration. After masturbating twice while lying next to Teresa—she touching him and loving him—Marty climaxed, allowing his sperm to fall on Teresa's stomach. (This was very important to Marty. He felt that he was closer and closer to being able to climax during penetration by giving his sperm to Teresa in this way. Sperm touching the woman's body seems to elicit a tremendous feeling of release in the male. He often reports a feeling of elation at seeing his sperm on his woman). Marty had this feeling and experienced it several times after that, enjoying it each time more and more.

Marty was now ready to climax while Teresa masturbated him instead of his masturbating himself. They engaged in a good deal of foreplay before Teresa successfully masturbated Marty to climax.

In all, Marty climaxed eight times during masturbation while close to Teresa. He ejaculated on her stomach and between her breasts, feeling that he had more and more control of "letting go" with each ejaculation. At last, he placed his penis between her thighs just as he felt about to climax, rubbing his penis for stimulation, and ejaculated between her thighs, very close to her vagina.

Marty and Teresa now felt ready for Contract IV, *the Full Sexuality Contract.*

The program which Marty followed has been described for your use. If you are unable to ejaculate during penetration despite the amount of time you thrust, if you cannot climax when you want to during oral sex or penetration, then you are a retarded ejaculator and should follow this program.

Like Marty, follow the desensitization process. After you have formulated Contract III, *the Non-Penetration Contract,* and have completed Chapters 6 through 9, begin the following procedure:

Love each other physically as you have been, using all of the sensuality and relaxation techniques which you have been enjoying. Excite each other physically and mentally, employing the turn-ons you both prefer, using fantasy, literature, massaging, or anything else you enjoy. When you would LIKE to climax, leave the room, and masturbate to climax. Do not wait. Do not apologize. Your contract is to achieve ejaculation when YOU CHOOSE TO. This is your mutual goal.

(If you do not have a permanent sexual partner, you still can follow all of these techniques. When you are with a partner who does not know about your problem, leave the room, making any excuse you need to. If you prefer, share your feelings with your partner and work together in this situation as you would with a permanent partner. Either way, leave the room and masturbate as described for a couple working together. Follow all the steps as described whenever you are with a partner. All of the exercises can be done on your own, but obviously you will need a partner to test your ability to ejaculate while with a partner.)

At your next lovemaking session, follow the same procedures, but this time, try to masturbate in the presence of your partner until you climax. If you can't do this, remain with your back to her, or have her look away. Your goal is to climax closer and closer to your partner each time.

When you have been able to masturbate to climax while your partner watches, you are ready to ask her to masturbate you to climax. You have masturbated:

(1.) Out of her vision.
(2.) While she is watching you.
(3.) While she is touching you.
(4.) She has masturbated you.

You are now ready to masturbate, or be masturbated, almost to climax and then quickly insert your penis between your partner's thighs—not into the vagina, merely between the thighs—and try to stimulate yourself to climax. You can do this by thrusting or by masturbating. Try to ejaculate as close to your partner's vagina as you can, but not IN the vagina, merely as close to it as you can.

This is one step away from penetration. Many men feel very threatened when they actually begin to penetrate. After climaxing successfully and ejaculating between their partner's breasts or thighs, they feel more confident about being able to "let go" during penetration.

Please remember that these steps must be followed in sequence. They are not to be done all at once. You cannot go from one step to another until you are securely successful with the one before. Go slowly. Be sure that you have secured one step before you reach for the next. Marty, for example, worked on his desensitization for about two weeks. Many men have stayed with desensitization for four weeks. It is up to you. Don't rush. Be patient. Build in as much success as you can by being sure, by not being impatient.

If you have completed all of these steps, you are ready for Contract IV, *the Full Sexuality Contract*, as described in Chapter 12.

For Marty and Teresa, the fourth contract read:

"We will engage in intercourse for as long as we both feel comfortable. If and when Marty feels he wants to withdraw to masturbate for a while or until he climaxes, this will be within his control. If at any time Teresa feels she would like thrusting terminated, she can control this, continuing with oral sex or masturbation."

This contract is personalized to Teresa's and Marty's desires. Other couples make far different contracts. Males have asked their partners to give up any control at all and allow them to decide whether or not to withdraw. If the female agrees, this is certainly feasible; in fact, it is advisable where possible. The male might be at the premonitory stage (just about to ejaculate) or close to it when the female asks him to withdraw. This would be destructive to a male feeling able to ejaculate during penetration for perhaps the first time. But it is also understandable that some women want the right to control the amount of time spent thrusting, since it can become painful or uncomfortable.

As you draw up your fourth contract, you must decide together how you want it to read. Remember, you are working for and with each other. Your primary goal is to achieve what BOTH OF YOU want. YOU must be flexible and creative enough to develop the contracts and the agreements that work best for BOTH OF YOU. There are an infinite number of possibilities.

For Marty and Teresa, therapy was very successful. Marty was able to ejaculate during penetration on his second attempt. At their first attempt, he was thrusting for longer than he wanted to and withdrew. Teresa masturbated him to climax immediately. During the second attempt, he ejaculated as soon as he decided he wanted to. The feeling he experienced was "pure ecstasy," he said.

Remember that you do not abandon one technique as you move on to another. Use everything you have learned throughout your entire program. Begin each lovemaking session with a form of relaxation exercise. Use the turn-on techniques you have discovered you enjoy the most. Pleasure each other fully.

When you attempt penetration, you should be at the height of excitement and pleasure. Do not rush this moment. Be patient. The more sensual you have been, the more loving and pleasuring you have had prior to penetration, the more likely you are to succeed. If you do not ejaculate when YOU WANT TO, which is your goal, do not worry. This merely indicates that you need more time. Withdraw and continue to masturbate to climax. You will succeed by continuing the program as designed. Take all the time you, personally, require. You may have to repeat the desensitization program, if you have worked too quickly or if you suffer a set-back during the program. But you will succeed by following this system—as so many others have.

When you are able to ejaculate WHEN YOU WANT TO during penetration, you have successfully completed "Help Yourself Sex Therapy." You have gained the control you want. You can now LET GO.

CHAPTER 16

Frigidity

THERE are some women who despite the type of stimulation, the area being stimulated, or any sexually arousing activity do not respond. Reading or viewing pornographic material, being touched or made love to, they do not respond.

They masturbate rarely, if at all. If they have tried masturbation, they have been unable to respond. There is no characteristic hardening of the nipples, moistening of the vaginal area, change of breathing rate, sense of excitement and arousal—none of these indicators are apparent.

Such women are sometimes called "frigid." Sex therapists know that this term is not only disparaging, but also that it has no *real basis in fact.* Such women are momentarily, temporarily, sexually dysfunctioning. Their therapy is as rapid and as sure as therapy for any other sexual dysfunction.

Janice called me on several occasions before really coming to the point. From the way she approached me, it was obvious that she was unsure of what she wanted from sex therapy and whether or not she could be helped. At first she pretended that she was calling about a "friend" of hers and gave me a false name. Eventually, she opened up a little.

One day, she mentioned that she "felt nothing" when it came to having sex with her husband. At this point, she finally asked me for an appointment and admitted that she wanted the help for herself.

I felt that she would benefit from beginning sex therapy on her own, to establish trust in herself and in the methods used. Women have only recently become aware of the fact that they are "entitled" to sexual pleasure. It is with great difficulty that some women announce that they DO want sexual pleasure.

151

It is even more difficult for them to feel that they deserve it. In our society it has been accepted that the man gets pleasure and the woman services him. Because of this, men are more ready to say, "Help me to have pleasure—there's something wrong," than are women. Most women still don't basically believe all this woman's movement stuff they keep reading about.

So it was with Janice. She is a modern woman, aware of the assertive behavior women are supposed to manifest, aware of her job rights, her home rights, her motherhood rights—all of them. But as aware as she was, she was still frightened to admit that sex was a foreign word to her. She didn't understand it, didn't register any feelings that she was aware of from the experience. She was terrified of any sexual encounter because of her inability to respond to and any physical attention. She accepted her husband's attentions as she would accept having a tooth drilled—something that had to be borne.

Janice began her therapy working alone at first. She began her treatment by first becoming acquainted with the entire program, as I hope you have. She then formulated Contract I, the *Non-Demand Contract*, and Contract II, the *Let's Really Try Contract*, promising herself that she would not expect too much of herself and that she wouldn't begin to feel like a failure if she didn't succeed immediately. She also agreed to work on her therapy for a minimum of one hour each day while her children were at school.

Janice and other sexually dysfunctioning women need to become aware of their own bodies and of their own arousal states to an even greater degree than do most men. Such women also profit a great deal when they explore some of their basic ideas about sex. They use the information for greater understanding about themselves and about what it was that caused them to turn themselves off to sexual joy and pleasure. Men can benefit from such exploration as well.

The following questionnaire is designed to be used by both sexes. I have chosen to put it in this chapter, because in my experience it has been the women who have asked for this type of information. I developed this questionnaire primarily because many women were having a hard time understanding themselves and their motivations.

Read the entire questionnaire before you answer any of the questions and then respond as honestly as you can. Try to be aware of your feelings as you read the questions. Are any, in particular, emotionally provocative to you? Are there questions which you think are disgusting? Ridiculous? Pointless? If so, please think about why you have judged them in this way. Respond slowly and carefully. Be as aware as you can of your feelings as you respond. Learn as much as you can about yourself:

(1.) Is sex disgusting?

(2.) Is sex neutral?

(3.) Is sex bad?

(4.) Is sex good?

(5.) Have you ever had intercourse?

(6.) What was it like?

(7.) Have you ever masturbated?

(8.) What was that like?

(9.) Did your parents make love with each other?

(10.) Did they enjoy lovemaking?

(11.) How do you know the answers to the last two questions?

(12.) Do you know—or did you guess?

(13.) What gives you pleasure?

(14.) What is your favorite part of your body?

(15.) What part do you most dislike?

(16.) What sexual act would you *never* want to do?

(17.) What sexual act would you *always* want to do?

(18.) What is most disgusting about men?

(19.) What is most pleasurable about men?

(20.) What is most disgusting about women?

(21.) What is most pleasurable about women?

(22.) Do you ever fantasize?

(23.) If yes, what are your fantasies about?

(24.) If no, why don't you?

(25.) What do you want from sex therapy (and from this book)?

(26.) What fantasy do you have about how you will be after you have completed the sex therapy exercises in this book?

(27.) Which of your answers above are lies?
(28.) Which are half-truths?

Please go back and correct your responses. Compare your second responses with your original ones. Go over the differences between them and uncover what you were hiding in your original responses.

This questionnaire must be treated most seriously. The responses you write are indicators to "where" and "what" you have turned off. To help you understand how to analyze the answers to this questionnaire, let's take a look at Janice's responses.

Janice completed the questionnaire in less than three minutes, writing "don't know" or "no" to almost every question. She had to be prompted to go over it again. This time she discovered a great deal about herself.

At first she had checked that sex was disgusting. As she examined the question more carefully, she admitted that somewhere in her mind she believed that sex was good, but since she didn't really know, her spur-of-the-moment response was that it was "disgusting."

She responded "no" to the question: "Have you ever masturbated?" Yet, upon further reflection, she stated that she did attempt touching herself on many occasions, but she failed to feel anything and was so frightened of being caught that she always stopped, feeling very ashamed and embarrassed. This despite the fact that she lived alone for two years before getting married. Even when she was in her own apartment with the doors locked, she felt she was being watched. Such irrational fears are not uncommon.

Although she answered "no" to both questions about her parents lovemaking the first time she completed the questionnaire, when she went back over it, she admitted that she was only guessing about what they did and whether or not they enjoyed it. She became aware of her own denial of sex—both the act itself and the sexual pleasure involved—even for others.

Janet realized that she could respond to *all* of the questions much more fully than she had the first time. This made her aware of a very important dynamic which was operating in her: "I don't even want to look at these areas, do I? I just push them away quickly, as if they don't exist."

Of course, she was right. Please, don't you push them away. Take your time. Answer the questions fully and honestly. Get as much information about yourself, for yourself, as you possibly can. Once a sexually dysfunctioning person learns to look at sex in all of its aspects—at least intellectually—that person is well on the way to solving his/her problem. Honesty is a first and very important step. With Janice's case, I learned the necessity of stating again and again how important it is to take this questionnaire seriously. In fact, it is essential that you take the entire program seriously to benefit as much as possible.

Janice began to pay attention to herself during her daily therapy hour. She followed the exercises in Chapters 6 through 9 carefully and conscientiously. She tape-recorded the exercises as directed and began to experience a sense of control. She was able to relax her body as she had never been able to before. She began enjoying looking at her own body without a sense of shame or embarrassment. She also learned to enjoy the touch of her own skin, and to experience various sensations:

(1.) She washed herself with her hands (rather than using the washcloth as she always had).

(2.) She rubbed herself with oil.

(3.) She smelled various parts of her body which she could reach with her nose.

(4.) She sucked on her own nipples by lifting her breasts up to her mouth and enjoyed the sensation. (If you cannot do this, suck on whatever parts of your body you can reach.)

(5.) She looked at her own body in the mirror for long periods of time without covering herself with her hands or a towel.

(6.) She touched herself as she watched herself in the mirror, enjoying it.

(7.) She looked inside her vagina with a small hand-mirror and examined herself as thoroughly as she could.

(8.) She found her own clitoris, and remarked (the next time she called me): "It's very pretty, small and hard and kind of proud-looking as it stands up there . . . all red and shiny."

(9.) She became proud of her body and the feelings she could experience with it.

Very important, Janice also learned to control her "sex muscle," as described in Chapter 4. She used this muscle as often as she could. This can be done easily. As you're riding in a car, on a bus or train, merely, "pull, pull, pull." You can feel the muscle as it contracts. When you're seated at the dinner table, or in the bathtub, pull, pull, pull.

After a while, tensing and untensing this muscle began to be more than an exercise for Janice. This is what usually happens and is a major reason why this exercise is so important. As she contracted the muscle, her entire vagina was contracting as well. This movement stimulated the little sweat glands in the vagina which began to secrete. Her vagina began to feel moist as it never had before. Janice was experiencing the excitement stage. If *you* are pulling on this muscle correctly after a time you, too, should feel a sense of wetness and excitement.

Janice found that if she contracted her vaginal muscle and licked her nipples at the same time, she became excited to the point of actually enjoying herself and feeling that she was nearing what "must be an orgasmic feeling," as she said.

She now felt ready to share her therapy program with her husband Paul. She told him everything that had happened since her first calls to me, including all she had experienced since beginning the program. He readily agreed to join her, and from then on they worked together.

They wrote new Contracts I and II replacing those Janice had designed for herself, working alone. Contract I:

"We will experience the sensate focus exercises together, giving each other as much support and attention as we possibly can, with absolutely no sexual activity between us."

"I, Janice, agree to be as honest as I can about my feelings, my needs, my pleasures, so that Paul can respond to me as fully as possible."

Janice added this last paragraph to Contsact II, the *Let's Really Try Contract,* feeling that it was important for her to verbalize her sincere desire to change. The rest of the contract read as follows:

"We both want to enjoy sex and we'll work toward that end

every evening from 9 to 10 P.M. We realize this is OUR problem, and we BOTH have the same goal—pleasure."

Paul wrote this contract and when he asked Janice if it was all right, you can imagine her joy at having him say that he felt it was not just HER problem, but a mutual situation which they both wanted to change.

In fact, Paul called me to say, "I'm the one who should have asked for help, since there's no such thing as a frigid woman. She's only as good as the man she's with. It's all my fault."

I immediately dispelled this damaging notion. As with any of the dysfunctions, it is essential that YOU realize there is NO blame, NO fault. Some people have more difficulty with sexual enjoyment than others—it is as simple as that. If you or your partner are suffering from a sexual hang-up, please begin to work TOGETHER so that BOTH OF YOU can benefit from these techniques and cures. Guilt, blame, shame—these feelings will only cause more pain and keep you from the true enjoyment possible.

Working together Paul and Janice continued to enjoy the exercises which Janice had already taped. Janice was by this time having a good many pleasurable sensations, since she had been working on her awareness alone. She knew what was pleasurable to her and when she shared this knowledge with Paul, he was able to give her pleasure and arouse her as never before. This, of course, was very positive for Paul, since he wanted to be able to stimulate and to please Janice.

Three weeks after they began working with *You Can Be Your Own Sex Therapist,* Janice and Paul had completed the program up to Chapter 11. Actually, they had completed the first ten chapters in two weeks but wanted to take an additional week to be sure. They were now ready for Contract III, the *Nonpenetration Contract.*

They were using all of the relaxation techniques during their lovemaking session and found that they both enjoyed fantasy. Paul began sharing his fantasies with Janice and they became very stimulated by this. They focused on image-making in their relaxation exercises as well as in their fantasies.

At the same time, Janice began doing other exercises on her own to help her toward her ultimate goal of an orgasm.

She began the following masturbation techniques to attempt to bring herself to climax. Before beginning any of these exercises, she always relaxed herself completely, bathing herself and touching herself as much as possible, as sensually as possible. Begin these exercises only when you feel you are ready. Be as comfortable as you can with your body, relaxed and sure of your own readiness:

(1.) Take the clitoris between two fingers and rub back and forth with the two fingers. Do this slowly at first, rubbing gently. Change the pace and the pressure as you want to.

(2.) Rub the clitoris with one finger up and down, or back and forth.

(3.) Use the entire hand over the vaginal opening with special pressure at the top, so that the clitoris receives most of the attention.

(4.) Use the entire hand and make circular movements at the top of the pubic area, directly against the pubic bone. (Place your fingers slightly below the hair line, and you'll feel the pubic bone.) Use your other hand to raise your breast to your mouth so that you can lick your nipple at the same time.

(5.) While taking a bath, lie back in the tub allowing the warm water to relax you. Put your legs up so that the water spout is directly over your vaginal area. Position yourself so that the water is falling directly where you want it, stimulating your clitoris. Many women find this especially pleasurable, since they can relax and enjoy it without tiring their hands. Please be sure the water doesn't go directly into your vagina but is falling on the clitoris.

(6.) Use a vibrator (available at any drug store). Do not insert the vibrator into the vagina (as many women mistakenly do) until you can first reach orgasm with clitoral stimulation. Allow the vibrator to "play" along your clitoris until you reach the orgasmic stage.

The use of vibrators is especially recommended and advisable if you are having trouble stimulating yourself through other masturbation techniques. Vibrators are wonderful adjuncts to good sex even after sexual fulfillment is achieved by physical means. Remember, anything which excites you and turns you on during your therapy should continue to be used and enjoyed throughout your sexual lives. Don't drop anything that brings you pleasure.

Janice became aware of what excited her most, what types of masturbation she enjoyed most and which brought her to orgasm more readily than others. She also noticed various degrees of intensity in her orgasms, and realized that some types of touchings were more effective for her than others.

Be as aware as you can of your reactions to the various masturbation techniques which you employ and use those which are best for you.

The descriptions of some masturbation methods does not mean that I frown on any other technique you may prefer. Be creative. Whatever delights you, as long as you don't endanger yourself, is right for you. But please don't insert bottles into your vagina. Don't use objects which are not clean. Don't place an object into your anus and then immediately into your vagina. Don't use electric appliances which are not specifically designed for masturbation. (I had a patient once who used an electric hair dryer, allowing the air to blow into her vagina.) These are very dangerous and should be avoided.

Janice continued self-stimulation and enjoyment of her

own body until she experienced an orgasm. This took place after three days of sexually stimulating herself for about an hour each day. Remember that Janice was also doing the relaxation exercises, exercising control of her "sex" muscle and becoming much more sensual following the exercises in Chapters 6 through 9.

Janice and Paul's third contract, the *Nonpenetration Contract* which they were now ready for, read this way:

"I agree to stimulate Janice in the ways she enjoys until she has an orgasm. After Janice experiences at least one orgasm, we will attempt mutual oral sex, or if Janice feels sated, other pleasuring experiences for me. If Janice prefers, she will stimulate herself to orgasm whenever she feels she wants to."

Janice continued to spend one hour each evening with Paul and approximately half an hour a day pleasuring herself and learning to exercise more and more control over her "sex" muscle. She and Paul abstained from penetration for almost two weeks, enjoying all other forms of sexual satisfaction. They then felt ready for the fourth contract, the *Full Sexuality Contract*:

"We agree to begin having intercourse whenever Janice desires. This will be within her control. We will both experience orgasm in any way we choose in addition to penetration, either before or after penetration."

This contract accomplished several things. Janice was in control as she should be since she was the partner with the dysfunction. She knew that she would not be deprived of orgasm by being limited to penetration alone. She also could choose whether to achieve orgasm before or after any attempt at penetration. Paul was also satisfied, since the contract clearly states that they would BOTH experience orgasm in any way they chose.

The most important element in this contract was that both Paul and Janice understood that their main goal was for Janice to experience orgasm and pleasure during penetration.

I am happy to report that Janice and Paul are now experiencing a very full and satisfactory sex life. Janice uses such adjuncts to her sexual experiences as pornographic literature and vibrators. Paul has become as involved as Janice with turn-on literature and stimulators and they both feel perfectly satisfied, changing their lovemaking from time to time.

When Janice first got in touch with me, she did not recognize, did not feel any of the characteristic sensations connected with sexual excitation. Now, she has learned many ways to stimulate these feelings. Fantasy, image-making, various types of touching or moving, can bring her to a state of high excitation.

Awareness has made this possible. Janice is now aware of these sensations simply because she has trained herself to become aware of them. She is now a pleasured and happy person. Paul is equally happy:

"We were two strangers, feeling our way through a maze of darkness we'd accepted as necessary and unavoidable. It's a new life for both of us, and although we know that we did it ourselves, we thank you so very much for showing us the way." (From a letter from Janice and Paul received eight months after they had completed *You Can Be Your Own Sex Therapist*.)

Not every woman who considers herself frigid is married to a loving husband like Paul.

Sylvia believed herself to be frigid when she began this therapy. She was 29, had never been married. She had avoided close contact with men, because she feared sexual relationships.

She followed the entire program exactly as prescribed here. She made Contracts I and II, the *Nondemand Contract* and the *Let's Really Try Contract*. She did as many of the exercises in Chapters 6 through 9 that she could without a partner. She also did the exercises in Chapter 3, controlling her sex muscle. In addition, she did all of the exercises in this chapter.

As she learned to relax and turn-herself-on using fantasy and physical stimulation, Sylvia became aware of the pleasures her body could experience. The more pleasure she achieved for herself, the more confident she became about herself as a woman.

Sylvia's first sexual experience was with a man whom she had known for only three weeks. Because she was attracted to him and because of her wonderful new confidence, she wrote Contract III, the *Nonpenetration Contract*, for herself, so that she could begin to experience some sexual feelings with a partner.

Sylvia introduced her man to the relaxation techniques she used, by playing tape recordings she had made of the exercises, and they both enjoyed them together, discussing their feelings afterwards.

Sylvia was fully able to control her "sex" muscle by now. She knew where to masturbate for the greatest arousal and could share her preferences with her companion. She shared her fantasies and image-making exercises with him as well, all of which he enjoyed.

Their lovemaking was sensual and pleasuring for the first three times they were together. She felt ready to execute Contract IV the *Full Sexuality Contract*.

Sylvia asked her lover to have intercourse with her. Later, she told me: "As the words came out of my mouth, I almost went into shock, I was so amazed."

Today, Sylvia's sex life is every bit as satisfying in its way as Janice and Paul's.

If frigidity is your problem, follow this program exactly as Janice and Sylvia did. To sum up:

Make Contracts I and II, the *Non-Demand* and the *Let's Really Try Contracts.* Commit yourself to the goal of achieving a more satisfactory sex life, and decide exactly when you will be able to do this.

Follow the exercises in Chapters 6 through 9, and master the techniques.

Complete the questionnaire in this chapter, learning as much as you can about yourself.

Do all of the exercises in this chapter. Learn to enjoy touching your own body and to masturbate.

Be able to bring yourself to climax utilizing all of these techniques.

When you are ready, make Contract III, the *Nonpenetration Contract,* then Contract IV, the *Full Sexuality Contract.*

Continue the exercises and techniques you have learned and which are bringing you new pleasure. No one has to be deprived of the pleasures of a fulfilling sexual life. These pleasures are now yours to enjoy. Use the knowledge you now have to give yourself pleasure and to share pleasure with someone else.

There is no end to the road of pleasure; it goes on as far as you care to walk it.

CHAPTER 17

Nonorgasmic Women

PAM had been reading a book about sex and came across a description of an orgasm. She noted that, during orgasm, a woman experiences certain characteristic physiological responses: hardening of the nipples, a spasm or spasms of the entire body, a total relaxation of tension, perhaps an instant of "blackout," or perhaps a slight chest rash, changes in her breathing, etc.

Pam was very upset and started phoning her friends, asking them what sex felt like to them. She didn't learn much. Most of her friends didn't want to discuss their intimate sexual feelings. But from what little she did learn, she understood that there were spasms of some kind or another and extreme tension in the muscles until the release during orgasm. One girl told her that her entire body rose up, her stomach stretching toward the ceiling, until her release.

Pam had never felt any of this. She had always thought of herself as very sexual. She was literally always "ready." She felt excited, her vagina was "wet," and she liked making love and did, often. Why, then, was she missing so much?

Pam was a nonorgasmic woman. This is very different from the frigid woman. As you can see, Pam experienced all of the physical sensations characteristic of sexual arousal. Her dysfunction came at the excitation stage: she never passed it.

It is not uncommon for women to fail to recognize that there is something missing from their sex lives. If they feel excited and enjoy the foreplay and sexual activities they engage in, they sometimes don't realize they are not climaxing. A nonorgasmic woman does not build up enough tension to want or need a release for it. She is constantly at the stage of feeling excited and good, in many cases. Some women believe that wetness in the vagina is due to orgasm. They believe they've climaxed. Other women think that if their vagina contracts, they have climaxed. Women like Pam often don't recognize that they have not had an orgasm, because they experience the pleasure and enjoyment of the excitation stage prior to orgasm.

When Pam came to see me, her attitude was angry and defiant: "I'm here to get a few facts, that's all. There's some stupid stuff I've been reading which has me confused and I want to get it straight."

I understood her confusion. Since she was enjoying sex and feeling fulfilled, I could imagine how frustrating it must have been for her to suddenly awake to the fact there was more out there which she had not even been aware of.

I already had proof that "Help Yourself Sex Therapy" could succeed for women with sexual dysfunctions. I asked Pam if she would be willing to follow the program and the written directions which I gave her. She said she would try.

At first Pam worked alone, not telling her husband, Howard, anything about her visit to me or the program she was following.

She executed Contracts I and II, the *Non-Demand* and the *Let's Really Try* contracts, and completed the questionnaire in Chapter 16. She also began the exercises in chapters 6 through 9, doing as many of them as she could on her own.

Pam tape-recorded all of the exercises and was able to listen to them and practice them over and over. After two weeks of working alone, she had learned how to masturbate herself to climax and experienced the first orgasm she had ever had. Pam was 31 years old at the time.

She was so excited and thrilled with her success that she told Howard about the program. After that, they worked together. They wrote Contracts I and II, combining them as follows:

"We will really try to learn as much as we can about how to improve our sexual life together. We will spend at least one hour a day every other day working together and will sincerely follow the program as it is outlined, taking full advantage of the experience and knowledge of the developer of the program."

(I appreciated the plug they put into the contract for me and for the program. As I've said again and again, please do follow this program closely and don't try to write your own. This one works.)

Pam and Howard worked together two weeks before they felt ready for the third contract. They continued using the recorder, taping their discussions regarding their experiences. They were so thrilled with the amount of communication these discussions brought out that they repeated the exercises over and over.

Howard was especially delighted with the depth of these exchanges: "We were so superficial in much of what we said, prior to this program, that it is hard to believe we stayed together so long when we were missing so much of the real person inside each of us."

Besides improved communication, there were other advantages. As is the case with many dysfunctional persons, the relaxation exercises were particularly important and particularly appreciated. Pam felt these exercises were the key to her ultimate success. She felt that without being able to "let go," as she learned to do using these techniques, her body could never have "let go" at the orgasmic stage. Before using these exercises, Pam could not keep her mind "quiet." She was always thinking, planning, indulging in make-believe conversations with people, going over problems, worries, and so on. The relaxing exercises helped her tremendously to clear her mind of this negative use of energy.

After Pam experienced her first orgasm, she became more and more aware of exactly what was taking place with her body. She realized that the more relaxed she was, the easier it was for her to bring herself to climax:

"As I got limper and limper—like a rag doll—using the fantasy techniques and my 'sex' muscle as I masturbated, my climaxing became more frequent, quicker and more intense."

Pam also used the relaxation exercises to help her to enjoy her own body. At first, she was very tense about masturbating and found it very difficult to touch herself with any pleasure at all.

I was pleased with Pam's success, because I have always stressed the importance of the relaxation techniques for everyone with sexual problems. I urge: "Please be sure to practice these exercises until you've mastered the art of a 'quiet mind and a quiet body.' Pam did this.

Exactly four weeks after she first began the program—two weeks of working alone and two weeks of sharing the experience with her husband—she and Howard were ready to formulate Contract III, the *Nonpenetration Contract.*

During the formulation of this contract, Howard rebelled against Pam's continuing to masturbate herself during their lovemaking. This is a very common problem which may arise in your own sex therapy. Many persons feel threatened when their partner masturbates during lovemaking. They feel that they are not satisfying their partner enough, or that the partner prefers to masturbate, rather than be made love to, or they have other, similar feelings of inadequacy and jealousy.

It is important that you remember that *all sexual approaches are wonderful and marvelous for both of you* as long as they are giving you pleasure. In Pam's case especially, as with all women who are having problems reaching climax, masturbation is very important.

When Howard understood the necessity for Pam's masturbation and discussed his feelings of being left out and rejected, it was much easier for both of them to continue with the program.

Pam understood Howard's feelings, and shared her own with him, assuring him that she preferred his making love to her, but explaining that at this point it was important for her to be orgasmic and to enjoy sex to its fullest as often as possible.

You must realize that you must have the use of any and all techniques which will help you to enjoy full sexual pleasure. Masturbation is one of these tools, for both men and women but especially for women with sexual difficulties.

After long discussions and thanks to the fact that they could now communicate more fully, Pam and Howard were able to resolve this problem. They were ready to continue their therapy experiences with Contract III, the *Nonpenetration Contract:*

"Pam and I will begin to experience sexual pleasure with each other, pleasuring each other in every way that we can. If either of us wants to pleasure ourselves, we will do so in the presence of the other while in physical contact with each other. We will make love in all ways other than sexual intercourse."

Howard wanted to be part of the masturbation process in whatever way he could. Pam's nipples were very sensitive; when they were stimulated, it excited her and brought her closer to orgasm. She asked Howard if he would lick and touch her nipples whenever she began to masturbate. He asked her to do the same if he masturbated or if she masturbated him. In this way they were both committed, contractually, to "be together" even when they were stimulating themselves.

They were involved in their third contract for just four days when both decided that they wanted to begin sexual intercourse. They wrote the following contract after three lovemaking sessions which did not include penetration, but did include all other sexual stimulation for both. They were both orgasmic each time.

Pam and Howard wrote the following for Contract IV, the *Full Sexuality Contract:*

"We will begin full sexual activities including sexual intercourse. Pam will initiate it when she wants to and be in control of stopping thrusting at any time. If penetration is stopped, we will climax in any other way we choose."

Pam felt that she needed to be able to stop if she wanted to, because she could not be sure that she would climax during penetration. Howard agreed with this as part of their common goal for their increased pleasure.

Pam feels that she owes her success in help yourself therapy to Howard and to the way in which he responded to her needs.

She was able to tell him the "hows and the wheres" of what she enjoyed. She felt free to ask him to masturbate her in certain ways, in certain places and ask him to have oral sex with her.

Howard, too, began to ask for specific types of lovemaking. He, too, felt more comfortable and open about expressing his needs and desires.

Pam and Howard have developed a lovemaking plan, following Chapter 10, the *Lovemaking Plan,* which is very satisfactory to both of them. Aware that Pam needs a great deal of relaxation before any sexual activity, they both do various breathing exercises which they have taped. They also find that dancing with each other is a good body loosener—and a very sensual experience when done by candlelight, in the nude. They bathe and shower together and massage each other, giving and taking pleasure as much as possible.

It is possible for a woman with Pam's problem to succeed with this program working alone. Unlike Pam, Lorrie didn't have a husband or a steady sexual partner. She spent most of her evenings alone when she started help yourself therapy. She was 26 and dysfunctional like Pam—but with a difference: Lorrie was able to experience orgasm when she was alone, but never when she was with a man. She became so tense and nervous that it was impossible for her body to let go.

Lorrie completed this program successfully, using all of the techniques the way Pam did. After three weeks of practicing the techniques in Chapters 6 through 9 alone, she decided to share some of the sensual exercises with one of her men friends.

Lorrie and her friend enjoyed the tapes which she played and derived a great deal of pleasure from them. Lorrie had taped the instructions regarding stimulating the senses with different fabrics, scents, types of touchings, etc., described in the chapter on sensuality and sexuality. She had also recorded the actual relaxation and image-making exercises.

They played one exercise for relaxation. They then listened to the tape on sensuality techniques. Lorrie brought out various materials and stimulated her lover as the tape played, touching him with velvets and silks, tickling him with feathers and offering him several scented objects.

It was the first real fun experience Lorrie had ever had, in a sexual context with a man. She was so pleasured and relaxed that she was prepared to take further risks with this lover.

She designed a third contract for herself after about two

weeks of sharing these various exercises with her lover. She began sharing her needs with him, her preferences, what her body responded to best—her most intimate desires. She was amazed at how responsive he was and how much he enjoyed their sexual meetings.

Lorrie formulated Contract IV, the *Full Sexuality Contract,* only three days after she had written Contract III.

Lorrie was successful, not only with the program which she followed exactly but with her ability to transfer her new awarenesses to a partner and enjoy all of the pleasures of her sexuality.

If you are working alone, be as creative as you can when you do decide to practice what you've learned with a partner. I have presented examples of various ways others have shared their experiences with partners. Use some of these ideas but be creative, find your own ways and means of sharing and achieving your sexual goals.

If you are non-orgasmic, or if you wish to increase the frequency of your ability to climax, follow the program exactly as Pam and Lorrie did:

Make Contracts I and II, committing yourself to the goal of achieving a more satisfactory sex life.

Complete the questionnaire in the chapter on frigidity, Chapter 16.

Follow all of the exercises in Chapters 4 through 9 and master the techniques.

Do all of the exercises in Chapter 16; learn to enjoy touching your own body and to masturbate.

Be fully able to bring yourself to climax utilizing all of these techniques.

"Life is so short, pleasures so few, thank goodness ours have increased a million times over." This is a quote from Howard. It's been said to me in other words and to hundreds of other sex therapists, thousands of times over, I'm sure.

Sex therapy works. YOU can change your levels of pleasure and increase your joys as much as you want to. Pam and Lorrie know this is true. You will, too, if you follow the program through, step by step, believing that you DESERVE all that you want from your sexual life.

CHAPTER 18

Vaginismus

NAOMI is 33. Married eight years, she had had a very satisfactory sex life for six of them. Suddenly, she began having a great deal of discomfort, experiencing pain during intercourse. Since they had made love for so many years with so much enjoyment, she and Don, her husband, couldn't understand what was happening.

Her gynecologist informed Naomi that the discomfort she was experiencing was due to a common infection known as vaginitis. But even after the infection was cleared, the pain Naomi felt during intercourse was unbearable.

She and Don kept trying to have intercourse, gently and carefully, but it was still painful; Don could not penetrate at all. The couple was confused and frightened—not knowing where to turn. Their solution was to try and ignore the problem, but their attempts at lovemaking were fewer and fewer until they were almost strangers to each other physically.

Don was hurt and angry. He didn't understand the situation and he was embarrassed to discuss it with Naomi, because he didn't want to hurt her any more. Naomi was as embarrassed as Don, but she felt responsible, so she didn't want to discuss it either. She certainly didn't want to continue attempts at lovemaking since the pain was, as she said, "excruciating . . . and would actually make me cry."

This situation had existed about three months when, one night, after a particularly good evening together, they began to make love. Don tried to insert his fingers into Naomi's vagina to stimulate her, but could not find the opening!

Naomi had vaginismus, a sexual dysfunction which actually causes the vagina to close up. Nothing can penetrate when this

173

occurs. It was as though a seal had been placed over what had once been a receptive and exciting doorway. Naomi was as frightened and confused as Don. She found that she couldn't insert a tampon, or even her finger.

Luckily, Naomi heard me speak on a radio program, discussing the work I do and called for an appointment. This call was made about two months after she had discovered her vagina had closed, almost five months after she and Don had stopped making love.

This was not an unusual situation. The problem is rare, so rare most people have never heard of it. Where the problem does arise, people are usually so frightened and confused that they will "ignore it" for months at a time. Where sex is infrequent and distasteful to her, the woman with vaginismus may not consider it a problem at all. She may not even be aware that her vagina has closed. Menstrual flows are normal and can pass through, so can the urine, so it's possible for vaginismus to go unnoticed. Only if you attempt penetration in some form—tampon, penis, finger—will the problem become evident.

Strange as it may seem, it can happen. In the book *The New Sex Therapy*, Dr. Helen Kaplan discusses a woman who had vaginismus and did not have sexual intercourse for the entire four and a half years of her marriage, at which point she was referred for treatment.

Such situations are extremely unfortunate. Vaginismus is a sexual dysfunction which can be cured, with the proper treatment, in a very short time. You don't have to suffer with this; you can lead a full and wonderfully passionate life, as Naomi discovered.

Naomi agreed to begin her treatment with "Help Yourself Sex Therapy." I gave her the information, the exercises and techniques, which you have read in Section II. I told her to proceed with them exactly as directed. I gave her permission NOT to indulge in any sexual activities for at least one month. I also suggested that she discuss the program with Don and involve him in it rather than work alone. (She could easily have begun this program alone, because it is successful for women regardless of whether or not they have a permanent sexual partner.)

I stressed to her—and to Don when he called me—that blame, recrimination, fault-finding, and accusation cannot help any situation. I explained that sex therapy is a two-way street when a couple is working together. They have a mutual goal: sexual satisfaction for both of them. They should always remember that they are aiming for that goal TOGETHER.

Don accepted this premise willingly, feeling, "Nothing happens in a vacuum. I'm as much a part of what happens to Naomi as she is of what happens to me."

They began treatment by formulating Contracts I and II, the *Nondemand* and the *Let's Really Try* Contracts. Here is their Contract I:

"We will work for a minimum of one hour a day, enjoying the exercises and learning the skills involved. We will not have intercourse for one full month. There will be no attempt at penetration. We will not have any sexual activities at all until we feel we are ready for them. We will have only sensual pleasures."

This contract did one very important thing for Naomi: it took away the pressure of her fear of penetration and pain. She knew that there would be no punishment for her inability to be penetrated . . . no guilt. This freedom from pressure, as I've already mentioned, is most important for those partners who are suffering from a sexual dysfunction.

Contract II for Naomi and Don read as follows:

"We know what we want and we're going to get it, by working together, enjoying all of the pleasures and looking forward to returning to a wonderful and complete sex life as soon as possible."

They were ready to begin the exercises in Chapters 6 through 9. Like most of the couples who tested help yourself therapy, they taped all of the exercises and listened to them together. This facilitated matters, since they were able to go through the exercises over and over until they had really mastered them.

They taped their discussions, learning a great deal about each other. Listening to the discussions, to the tone of voice of the responses, as well as to the content, they could really "hear" themselves and understand each other better.

In addition to these exercises, Naomi was practicing

strengthening her "sex" muscle as described in Chapter 3, *Put Power In Your Sex Muscles.* Before long, she was able to feel her vagina lubricating inside and could feel that it was more relaxed, looser.

When she felt relaxed enough—using the relaxation exercises, then contracting her sex muscle to relax and lubricate her vagina—Naomi was ready to begin the desensitization program essential to curing vaginismus.

For this you need a series of six to ten plastic tubes, about five or six inches long, ranging in size from a half inch to two inches in circumference. These can be purchased at a plastics supply store or substitutes can be used—sterilized cocktail stirrers, lipstick tubes, tampons, the cardboard around the tampon, plastic straws, etc. Any tubes will serve as long as they are of graduated thickness and absolutely clean.

Naomi began the desensitization program by inserting the narrowest tube. She removed it and attempted to insert the next size tube. I had advised her not to insert the cylinder completely at first. Insert it into the mouth of the vagina and

gradually go as deep as you can, being sure to keep hold of the object.

Naomi did these exercises in private, without Don. She kept the tape recorder on playing the breathing exercise, because this relaxed her. She always made sure, too, that her vagina was lubricated by contracting her sex muscle. (If this doesn't lubricate you well enough, please be sure to use petroleum jelly or whatever lubricant you usually use.)

Naomi completed this part of the program by the end of the second week of treatment, spending about forty minutes a day on the desensitization exercises. In addition, she and Don allotted one hour a day together, going over the techniques in Chapters 6 through 9.

They were both enjoying the exercises and feeling loving and warm toward each other for the first time in many months. There had been so much anger and resentment between them for so long that they had forgotten how to be kind to each other. Servicing and pleasuring each other during the sensate focus exercises brought back the wonderful feelings they had shared before the vaginismus developed.

They began the sexual sharing exercises in Chapter 9. At the same time Naomi was ready for the next step in her desensitization program. After successfully inserting all of the tubes and being able to move them in and out of her vagina without discomfort as well as moving them around, stretching the opening of the vagina gently and slowly, Naomi heeded the following instructions:

I told her to insert her own fingers into her vagina and move them around inside. She was to begin with one finger and proceed by increasing to two, then three, fingers.

Meanwhile, Naomi and Don continued with the treatment procedure, mastering all of the techniques up to Chapter 9. They were ready to formulate their third contract. Contract III, the *Nonpenetration Contract* read as follows:

"We will resume all sexual activity other than penetration after several exercises—including relaxation and image-making—then beginning sexual stimulation."

Naomi was now beginning to feel very excited and eager to make love again. One day, during a relaxation exercise, Don was telling her a fantasy as he massaged her when she asked him to attempt to penetrate her vagina with his fingers, as she had been able to do with her own. This was so successful that she had the first orgasm she had experienced in six months.

If you suffer from vaginismus, or any sexual dysfunction, it is essential that you follow the nonsexual part of your Contracts I and II. A woman with vaginismus is easily orgasmic from clitoral stimulation. The fact that the mouth of the vagina has closed does not interfere at all with her ability to climax; but the male cannot penetrate. He is deprived of one of the most exciting forms of sexual pleasure. The woman is being deprived, too, since penetration is a pleasure for both.

So please be sure that there is *no sexual activity at all* for the entire time you require to complete all of the necessary techniques in Chapters 6 through 9, and for the female to penetrate her vagina successfully with the tubes or other objects and then with her own fingers. You can begin with your fingers, if you prefer not to use any objects, but, please, go very slowly and gently. Sexual activity is essential or the female may be less motivated to relieve her dysfunction if she continues to have orgasms through clitoral stimulation.

Naomi and Don were both orgasmic using all types of sexual stimulation other than penetration and were quite satisfied with their progress so far. Naomi was not experiencing any pain at all during finger penetration, nor was she at all frightened when Don approached her vaginal area.

Naomi experienced what I've described to you in other situations: the step-by-step process called "desensitization." As she inserted one tube after the other, each one a little larger than the one before, her vagina was being conditioned to accept the new penetration. The sensation was not uncomfortable or unpleasant, because Naomi had full control of what was going on. She trusted herself not to hurt herself, and so she could proceed without fear.

By this time, Naomi and Don were very aware of their excitation states and of what excited them most. They were using all of the turn-on techniques and the relaxation exercises which they found pleasurable and helpful. They were enjoying sexual activities and experiencing orgasms through oral and manual stimulation.

When all of this had been achieved successfully, when

Naomi was able to penetrate her vagina first with objects, then with her fingers and, finally, Don's fingers, Naomi and Don were ready for Contract IV, the *Full Sexuality Contract:*

"We will use all of the methods available to us to become as passionate as possible. Then we shall attempt penetration. We will try for partial insertion at first, but if complete insertion is possible, we shall continue slowly. Naomi will be in full control of when to stop, how to continue, what position to use and what movements we'll make. Regardless of whether we withdraw or not, we'll continue with sexual play until we both climax."

By using a great deal of foreplay and fantasy to create the heights of passion they wanted to reach, Naomi and Don achieved penetration partially on the first attempt and completely on the second. Actual thrusting did not take place until their third lovemaking experience. Don remained quietly inside Naomi during the first two penetrations. When he did begin to thrust, it was very gently and slowly, to avoid hurting her.

Naomi has been free of any dysfunction since the completion of her treatment. She and Don have been making love successfully with no problem whatsoever.

Despite the severity of this dysfunction, there seems to be a high rate of success in its treatment. Following the step-by-step program prescribed, allowing each other the freedom of choice of action during treatment, respecting and loving each other, working for and with each other, remain aware of what your goals are, and be deserving of them—all of this is important to the success of help yourself therapy.

Karen was able to cure her vaginismus dysfunction with this program, although she worked alone. Karen is 27. Her husband walked out on her, leaving her with two children. When she met someone else and attempted sexual intercourse with him about a month after separation from her husband, she discovered that her vagina had closed. She had never heard of vaginismus, of course, and imagined that the most terrible disease in the world had attacked her.

She was lucky, because her family doctor knew what her problem was and immediately referred her to sex therapy. She was sent to me by a women's center in New York. I asked her to begin *You Can Be Your Own Sex Therapist,* feeling that she could easily follow the program and benefit from it without having the expense of a therapist which she could not really afford.

Karen began by formulating Contracts I and II and making the commitments to herself which they required. She did all of the exercises in Chapters 6 through 9 which she could do on her own, taping the exercises and experiencing as much as she could of all of the techniques. She completed all of the questionnaires.

When she was with a partner, she played the relaxation exercises for him and they both enjoyed them. She abstained from all sexual activity until she had successfully completed the desensitization process and mastered all of the exercises in Chapters 4 through 9. This took her about two weeks.

Here is a breakdown of the program I asked Karen to follow:

Read through the entire program.

Follow all of the directions in Chapters 4 through 9 and master the techniques completely.

Follow the desensitization program in this chapter until you can easily and comfortably insert all of the objects, your own fingers, and, eventually, your partner's fingers (if you work with a partner).

Formulate Contract III, the *Nonpenetration* Contract, when you have satisfactory sexual experiences, can be penetrated with digital stimulation, enjoy climaxing, and are secure enough to attempt penetration.

Formulate Contract IV, the *Full Sexuality* Contract, following Chapter 12.

Begin penetration, slowly and gently. Begin with partial penetration, with a quiet penis, not moving at all. Penetrate further and move gradually until full penetration and thrusting is achieved.

At this point, you have successfully completed "Help Yourself Sex Therapy." Karen also successfully completed her program. She was able to share her problem with a man she had been seeing for a while, but with whom she was not having any sexual activities. They shared all of the exercises which she had taped. When she felt ready, after she had completed the desensitization program, she asked him to stimulate her internally with his fingers. They proceeded to penetration after two lovemaking sessions. This was completely successful after three partial insertions.

Karen did not suffer from her inability for very long. She was cured in less than four weeks from the time she visited her family doctor. At the Institute for Behavior Modification in New York, the director, Dr. Barry Lubetkin, who was kind enough to share his technique of desensitization with me, reports cures for vaginismus with weeks of treatment. "Since the woman does much of the work on her own, it's up to her to determine how long it will take her to desensitize herself," Dr. Lubetkin said during an interview on my television show, "Awareness with Carole Altman."

Whether you go to a therapist, a clinic, or use this program, YOU must do the work yourself. Sex therapy is based on the HOMEWORK principle. I can tell you what to do and how to do it, but it is up to you to go home and DO IT. This program is here for you, at no expense other than the cost of this book. USE IT. ENJOY IT. Your dysfunction will be a thing of the past. Pleasure will be your future.

Section IV

"FORBIDDEN" SEX

CHAPTER 19

Variety is the Spice of Life:
Specials and Turn-Ons

"I hope you can take care of my kind of problem, because I'm really in trouble. . . ."

"I'd be perfectly happy but my wife keeps complaining, so I guess we'd better get some help. . . ."

"Do you take care of very sick people? Because I'm very sick. . . ."

These are actual quotes. Each of these people felt they needed help, because their sexual tastes were slightly "different" from those of people they knew or had heard about. Each considered himself/herself to be "sick," because each wanted something "special."

Most of us, whether we admit it or not, want that something special. How many men say they are "breast men"? How many women can't respond to fat men? How often do we talk about chemistry or "a feeling," or "atmosphere"?

When we restrict our sexual enjoyment to a certain type of person, situation, physical attribute, or even time of day, we are limiting our experience. But such well-defined needs are not necessarily problems. They are our personal choice. We don't even realize how we have limited ourselves—or why.

In our society we have a consensus of "normal" or "healthy" behavior patterns. If everyone else does it, then it's "normal." If "they" (whoever "they" may be) don't do it, the behavior is labeled "abnormal" or "sick" when actually it's only nonconformity.

I revolt against the conformist concept. The need to compare to others, to have approval for behavior and to be like everyone else is, in many ways, less sane than varying your behavior and being creative and unique. Thoreau said it beautifully when he wrote, "March to the music of a different drummer." Our modern humanists say, "Different strokes for different folks."

This is my basic philosophy. Whatever tune you are dancing to is perfectly delightful, as long as you are not stomping on someone else as you dance and as long as you are not kicking yourself.

So if you are worried about what others would say, if you are ashamed to share your desires with a loved one, so that you can both enjoy the pleasures involved, if you judge yourself "strange" for some reason, let me assure you that you do not have an insoluble problem. You can learn to open up lines of communication and share with someone else. You can discover that you are entitled to certain behavior which you enjoy even though others may not share your taste.

If, however, there is more pain than pleasure in your behavior, if there is danger involved, if your activities are physically harmful, then, yes, you do have a problem.

You Can Be Your Own Sex Therapist can be used to rid you of your problem—if it is a problem. A few case studies from my files should help you to understand how:

Ann came to me, saying, "I hope you can take care of my kind of problem, because I'm really in trouble."

My first question was, "How does this problem manifest itself?"

"You mean, what is my problem?" she asked.

"No," I said, "I mean, how do you *know* it's a problem?"

I cannot stress this distinction strongly enough: How do you know it's a problem? Is it a problem because other people say it is? Is it a problem because you're embarrassed about it? Is it because you feel others will think you're strange? Is it because you enjoy it too much? If the answer to any of these questions is yes, is it really *your* problem?

Ann is a professional woman in her late twenties. She has two children and has been married for eight years. She is described as chic and talented by those who know her. Her view of herself is that she is perfect—or should be: keeping a perfect home, raising perfect children, being perfect in her profession. Her "problem" stood out to her like a sore thumb, because it was so at variance with her own high expectation of herself and with the expectations of others.

She was stunned by my question. "How do you KNOW it's a problem?" I repeated.

"Because it is . . . no one else does it . . . it's embarrassing. I wouldn't even do it with my husband, only with transient lovers—men I'll never see again. I'm so ashamed of it."

"Then it's a problem because you're ashamed of it?"

"No!" She was almost shouting. "It's a problem because it's wrong!"

We pursued this conversation until Ann realized that "wrong," "shame" and "sick" were all labels which she had put on this behavior of hers because it did not fit the accepted pattern of behavior in her "circle." It was different, unusual and unexpected, certainly, but was it sick, shameful or wrong?

Before asking what the behavior was, I insisted that Ann explore these questions in her own mind. I introduced her to help yourself therapy and had her begin—as everyone does— by writing Contracts I and II. I also outlined the exercises in Chapters 6 through 9 and asked her to start on them as soon as she got home.

At this first meeting, I also handed Ann the questionnaire below. I recommend it to anyone who is enjoying a certain type of behavior which he/she is secretly ashamed of:

Who says it's a problem?
Does it hurt anyone?
Is it fun?
Does it give you pleasure?
Does it give others pleasure?
Is there any danger involved in practicing it?
Do you wish you could stop this behavior?
Do you wish you could share it with someone?
Would you take the risk of sharing it?
What would happen if you did share it with someone? (If possible, have a particular person in mind when answering this question.)
What is the worst thing that could happen?
What is the best that could happen?
What will he (or she) say? Think? Do? (Visualize all the

possibilities. Face them now, privately and silently, without any real risk. Fantasize the responses, the behavior as you share your "problem.")

How would you feel?

How do you feel now as you think about the possibilities?

Is your behavior really "sick" or "wrong?"

Will you OWN it as your own creation, uniquely yours?

Are you depriving someone else of pleasure by not sharing it?

Will you OWN the pleasure you derive from it?

Do you DESERVE the pleasure you derive from it?

Will you take the risk of getting this pleasure more often?

If you have answered all of these questions and if, in your opinion, your behavior seems dangerous, unhealthy or one you wish to rid yourself of for any reason whatsoever, please see Chapter 20 where I explain the situations which require professional help. Also, read the desensitization techniques described in this chapter to help shed this behavior. There are other desensitization techniques outlined in Chapter 15, *Retarded Ejaculation,* and Chapter 20, *Forbidden Sex,* which you may find useful.

After Ann completed the questionnaire, she said, "When I look at it this way, it seems so different."

She then explained her troublesome behavior. She enjoyed behaving like a wild beast. She most preferred being a lion, growling and jumping around on the floor or bed, pretending to attack her lover. She would make faces, use her hands as paws and make rumbling sounds. She would struggle, fighting and pulling, squeezing and hugging as she attacked.

Ashamed to share such behavior with her husband, yet unwilling to lose the pleasure she got from it, Ann would pick up men for one-night-stand affairs. Afterward, however, she felt so guilty at betraying her husband, it took what pleasure she derived from the experience.

Ann had come to me originally with the hope of ridding herself of this behavior. But after she completed the questionnaire, she told me this story:

One night she was in a motel with a man whom she had picked up in a bar. As he was undressing, she began to pretend to be a lion, growling, running around and jumping. He became so frightened that he dressed rapidly and fled from the room. Several months later, she met the same man in a bar. It turned out that a friend of his had had a sexual encounter with Ann. The friend had told him that she was a great lover and that the evening had been the most exciting sexual experience he had ever had.

Telling me this, Ann realized that perhaps she was actually depriving her husband of the sexual pleasure and joy other men had with her when she was able to "let herself go" and express herself in the form of a lion.

She was afraid, though, that her husband would have the opposite reaction. She decided, however, to take the risk when she realized that it is not a sickness to pretend and to play in the bedroom.

Ann realized that she was not ashamed of her fetish—she was ashamed of her transient affairs. What she really wanted to do was to share her animal-play with her husband. She told him that she wanted to enhance her sexuality and that she had several exercises to follow to accomplish this. Together they reformulated Contracts I and II. When they came to Chapter 9, *Sexual Sharing*, Ann was able to tell her husband about her desire to act like a lion. To her joy—and relief—he was delighted to act out her fantasy.

When they were ready, she and her husband completed Contracts III and IV, agreeing to continue with sexual play, fulfilling each other's wishes in their sexual and sensual activities.

Ann was the type of a person who responded very strongly to pressures put on her by society as she was growing up, so strongly, in fact, that she could not let go unless she hid behind a mask.

Many of us devise ruses and masks behind which we can hide to let off some of our real feelings. We may change our voices, for instance, when we say loving things . . . haven't you ever noticed someone switching to "baby talk" to say "I love you" or "How pretty you look!"? Our voices change, too, when we are angry. Try saying, "Stop," or "I don't like it," and notice how your usual inflection alters. Some people's tone changes completely when they ask for something.

Often people will not play games, such as rolling down a hill, or building a sand castle or frolicking in the snow, unless a child is present. Then they have a socially acceptable excuse: they are "playing with the child." If you think about it, I am sure you can name a friend or two like this. Maybe even yourself.

In Ann's case, to be wild and free, to really let herself enjoy sex to the full, she hid behind the mask of a lion. As the lion, she was able to be uninhibited. This is perfectly normal, wonderful and exciting. There is no reason why we shouldn't wear masks and change identities from time to time. We can be that much more exciting to ourselves and to others. If we can express ourselves freely without the aid of "let's pretend," that is even more wonderful and exciting.

Ann eventually grew to accept, and truly enjoy her behavior and include it into her sexual repertoire. But Sidney, however, was desperate to shed his. He told me: "Look, I just want to get rid of one habit. I don't need a long, drawn-out deal, but it's really a horrible habit."

He said this before even introducing himself. He and his wife, Gloria, were in my office because she had convinced him that there was something wrong with their sexual practices.

I asked Sidney and Gloria to complete Contracts I and II. I gave the exercises and techniques in Chapters 6 through 9 to them to follow. I then asked Sidney to complete the questionnaire in this chapter which he did. His answers indicated that he felt there was nothing wrong with his "habit," except that his wife didn't like it. Gloria's answers to the questionnaire indicated her pleasure was "none at all," and that she felt his behavior was "sick."

Sidney's problem? He could not achieve an erection unless Gloria had all of her clothes on—with the exception of her panties—and unless he repeated "turn-on" words to himself over and over.

I asked if they would be willing to try *You Can Be Your Own Sex Therapist.* Both agreed.

Ann did not have to change her behavior, only learn to share it with her husband. In this case, Gloria was adamantly opposed to wearing clothes during lovemaking. Sidney's desires deprived them both of a great deal of sensual and sexual pleasure. His behavior would have to change.

I prescribed Chapters 6 through 9, advising them to take plenty of time enough to master the techniques and exercises. When they were ready for Contract III and sexual activity, Sidney began the following desensitization process. This procedure, which I have developed, can be applied to most behavior you might care to shed. If there are serious psychological problems involved in the behavior, or if there is a physical impairment causing the behavior, this procedure will not succeed. I suggest, in such cases, that you seek outside help. But for simple habits, fetishes or inhibitions, this process has been successful for many persons:

DESENSITIZATION PROCESS

(1.) Write a description of the behavior which you wish to change.

(2.) List all of the steps involved in this behavior as you practice it.

(3.) List all of these steps again, in the order of their importance to you.

(4.) From the list above, fantasize what it would be like to make love without the last step on the list being present.

(5.) Now fantasize what it would be like making love without the next to last item on the list being present.

(6.) Continue this fantasy until the entire list has been dispensed with as you fantasize making love without any of these things.

(7.) Actually make love without the last item on your list. Share your feelings about this with your partner.

(8.) If you completed number 7 successfully, make love without the next to last item on the list.

(9.) Continue this way, working your way up from the bottom of your list, until you can make love without any of the items you have listed.

The following is Sidney's list—and his description of how he succeeded in his help yourself therapy:

(1.) I wish to make love without any clothes on from now on.

(2.) I curse a lot, I make sure my wife is wearing all of her clothes, I ask her to remove her panties, I penetrate and begin thrusting to climax.

(3.) A. Cursing.
  B. Stockings.
  C. Brassiere.
  D. Slip.
  E. Dress.
  F. Hairpins.

(4.) (5.) and (6.) I was easily able to fantasize making love without items B through F. I didn't experience any problem until I tried to get rid of item A.

(7.) and (8.) We were able to make love without penetration without all of the clothing, and Gloria began using a lot of the exercises in Chapters 6 through 9 as well, so that we really enjoyed the touching and all.

(9.) In talking about this, Gloria realized that cursing wasn't so terrible. We began using your suggestions about using turn-on literature and stuff, so we have really incorporated all of this into our lovemaking.

Sidney and Gloria worked for five days under Contract III, without penetration, following all of the procedures in the desensitization process. They were then ready for Contract IV. They made love with penetration approximately one time without each successive item—once with Gloria's hair completely loose, once without her wearing her dress or hairpins, once without her wearing her slip, dress or hairpins.

The process of desensitization can be applied to many forms of behavior. Some may take longer than others, and, of course, some may be more difficult to shed than others. I have found, however, that if you truly care to experience more pleasure, if you take yourself seriously and work on your problem faithfully following the recommended procedures, you can succeed.

When Sandra called and said, "Do you take care of very sick people? Because I'm very sick," I wasn't sure what she meant, or if she was a candidate for sex therapy at all. But then she explained that she enjoyed sex only rarely. She told me that unless her partner took elaborate pains to decorate the apartment with candles, music, pillows, the right wines, satin sheets, vibrators, turn-on literature—everything that she had read about in books and magazines—she couldn't get aroused and would have no pleasure at all. The more she read, the more she demanded of her partner, and the relationship was falling apart.

Sandra was seeking a great deal of attention and proof that her partner loved her. At the same time, she was being self-destructive, since she could hardly ever have the perfect atmosphere and the perfect situation. Real life just isn't this way.

By following steps 1 through 9 of the desensitization process when she came to Contract III and by discussing the situation with her partner, Sandra discovered that he was willing to work with her and for her and gradually released him of many of the demands she had placed on him.

They still create a romantic atmosphere and enjoy it, but now they plan together, for each other, not just to satisfy Sandra's limitless demands. They use the Lovemaking Plan in Chapter 10 and have a lot of fun deciding on their own. Sandra enjoys her sexual life as never before. She realizes that all her demands were merely an expression of her insecurity and her need to have "proof" that her lover cared for her. She also realized that she was not "sick" and had never been "sick."

There are a multitude of special desires people need fulfilled before they can gain sexual release. Men may wear women's clothing, or vice versa. Some pretend to be raped or to rape; still others need the touch of certain types of fabrics, the right sounds, equipment.

Whatever your thing is—if you have one—remember that if you get more pleasure from it than without it, if you don't cause pain or damage to yourself or others, if you can share it with someone else and enjoy it together, or if you can enjoy it on your own, do so. Special desires are not necessarily dirty words. It is up to you to decide whether or not you want to keep yours.

CHAPTER 20

Inhibitions — To Have
or to Shed

INHIBITIONS are often considered commendable. How often have we heard: "Oh, isn't she sweet, she's so shy," or, "He's always blushing—he's so cute!" Our society is comfortable with the withdrawn, the somewhat shy and retiring type. We even foster this sort of behavior. We've all overheard mothers telling their children, "Pull down your dress," or, "Don't touch that, it's dirty."

Books are banned, movies are censored, people are arrested for writing erotic poetry and sending it through the mails. Most offenses against our society center around sex. We never hear of anyone being arrested because they send literature dealing with violence through the mails, or for selling war toys to children. But talk about sex in any way but the "accepted" way and the ax will fall.

Our society creates hangups, inhibitions, restraints, fetishes, embarrassments and withdrawals in the area of sex. The magnificent world of sex. The world of joy and pleasure . . . of delicious release from tension and trouble. The world of giving and receiving which cannot be expressed or experienced in any other way.

Sex . . . withheld from so many because of mistaken morals, judgments, disturbances in our upbringing and lack of information. We have been deprived of the joy of learning that sex is "super." But it is not too late. The restrictions which our society has placed on your psyche can be removed.

I have worked with many persons suffering from such restrictions. Their cases are exciting, because they have worked themselves out of their "problems" and are now

194

mature, sexual beings with no restrictions on their joy. Ellen is one of them:

Twenty-three-year-old Ellen had a good mind, a fine figure, a pretty face. On the surface, she was a happy woman, fulfilled in her choice of career, contented with her life, planning to be married within the year.

But despite two years of analysis and other therapy, including hypnosis, Ellen had a problem she could not resolve. She could not stand to be touched by anyone in any way except a simple handshake. When someone put an arm around her, touched her on the shoulder or accidentally brushed up against her, she would break out in a cold sweat. She would become so tense that a vein on the side of her head would begin to throb noticeably. She was afraid that she might have a stroke one day because of her unreasonable fear. When she came to me, she was suffering from insomnia. When she slept, she had nightmares about sex and marriage and was considering breaking her engagement.

Ellen needed to learn how to relax and to trust her own control of her bodily functions. Using the exercises she learned to relax her body and to control her tension. She completed Contracts I and II and worked on the appropriate exercises in Chapters 6 through 9, taping them and using them to increase her ability to relax.

As soon as Ellen was able to relax at will—after about a month—she began the desensitization process detailed in Chapter 19.

Ellen began the program exactly as described in the chapter. She first used fantasy, imagining that she was being touched in various areas of her body. She played the tapes of relaxation exercises during these fantasies. She imagined that many people were touching her, that one person was touching her, even that she was being attacked and her body abused. Throughout all of these fantasies, she was able to remain calm.

After about two weeks of this training, Ellen began touching herself as she had never done before. She used many of the exercises in Chapter 16, learning to masturbate and enjoy her own body. In another week, she was ready to have someone else touch her and introduced her fiancé to the program.

They formulated Contracts I and II and began working together, beginning with Chapter 6, completing all of the exercises, etc., through Chapter 9. At the same time, Ellen continued with the desensitization program in Chapter 19, slowly, gradually, being touched by her fiancé. First he touched parts of her body with which she was most comfortable and, finally those where she had the most difficulty being touched.

Ellen played tapes of the relaxation exercises and was able to keep calm. She did not proceed to the next area of her body until she was completely relaxed about being touched on the last one. Soon she was able to report that she not only remained relaxed when her fiancé touched her, but that she was enjoying it.

Within one week of daily practice they had been able to lie nude with each other. Ellen had asked her fiancé not to touch her with his hands, but merely hold her in his arms, their nude bodies close to each other.

They continued working for two weeks. Each day Ellen's fiancé escalated the types of touching behavior, starting with parts of her body she was comfortable with. During this phase, they kept the tape-recorded relaxation exercises playing as they touched, so that Ellen was assured of remaining relaxed. When she was able to not only tolerate being touched but actually enjoy it, they were ready for Contract III.

They formulated Contract III, *Nonpenetration,* and began the sexual exercises. They continued all of the earlier exercises, adding mutual masturbation, oral sex and other sexual activities. Each of these had to be introduced slowly, following the desensitization procedure. Ellen was truly enjoying sexual stimulation. She was also experiencing climax with manual stimulation.

Ellen told me later, "Once the first touch had been made, it was downhill all the way." They worked slowly, taking their time and being very patient. Ellen now felt very confident and eager to experience sexual intercourse. At the end of about two weeks, they moved on to Contract IV, *Full Sexual Activity.* Ellen enjoyed penetration. By combining masturbation and other foreplay techniques, she was orgasmic.

Ellen has been married two years now, with no report of any recurrence of her problem. She does not experience any of her old symptoms; people can touch her, be near her, even put their arms around her. She is not a "kissing" person and is still shy of very demonstrative people. But this is not unusual and is not a problem for her. Ellen now lives a normal, happy life. I received a letter from her recently. She is pregnant and wrote a short poem about it, one I recommend to every parent, or future parent:

"I'll touch my baby in loving ways . . .
All the nights and all the days."

Ellen's case is an example of an extreme inhibition. It required real concentration and determination on her part to succeed in help yourself therapy. Any inhibition that stands in the way of your pleasure or enjoyment is one you can rid yourself of. But it is up to you to decide whether or not you want to. Not all inhibitions are negative of course. For example, many people are inhibited against homosexual sex. You may choose to maintain this, as you may also choose to maintain an inhibition against group sex, or bisexual sex, or going to nude massage groups.

But there are many inhibitions which can deprive you of "happy sex" and keep you from being a free and sensual being who can "let go." We all have limitations, barriers, doors which are closed to us and which we choose to keep that way. What you must do for yourself is to decide if any of these closed doors are closing off pleasure for you, keeping you from fulfillment and restraining you in ways which you really haven't chosen. If you have such "closed doors," ones which you'd like to open, then please think about using the desensitization program in Chapter 19. You probably can shed this inhibition, as Ellen did, as so many others have been able to do.

Persons who don't enjoy certain sexual activities often ask my opinion about their "hangups." But such questions are among the most difficult to answer:

"Should I like being touched on my nipples? I really don't like it at all."

"What if I can't stand being penetrated when my husband is behind me?"

"What about oral sex? I hate it. Should I change?"

To this type of question I usually say this:

We have many choices in life, millions upon millions of choices. You can look at these choices as doors which are either closed or open. You choose which. You choose whether to marry or not, whether to have children or not, whether to be a doctor, a teacher or a carpenter. You decide which doors to open. You decide whether to smoke pot, to drink or gamble. You have control over whether you will have sex with only one person in your lifetime, or whether you'll have more than one partner. You decide if "switching" is for you, if you want orgies, multiple relationships, or open marriages. These are all doors which you decide to open or not.

There is an infinite variety of sexual practices and you will not open the door to all of them. You will decide to keep some of these doors closed. On the other hand, if you feel that you'd like to open a door which has been previously closed to you and take the responsibility to experience the situation openly and freely, you can do this too.

One sexual practice which many persons are inhibited about is oral sex. This can be an extremely enjoyable experience, an integral part of your sexual life. I have developed a very simple procedure to help you become more comfortable with oral sex and enjoy the pleasures of it. If you choose to open this door—and only if you choose to—follow these procedures with your partner.

Begin after you've had some relaxation exercises and feel close physically and mentally:

(1.) Begin to kiss any part of the body which you like to kiss other than the face. Keep your lips closed as you kiss that part of the body.

(2.) Continue kissing the same part of the body but this time open your mouth slightly and allow your tongue to touch the skin.

(3.) When—and only when—you are comfortable kissing, then begin actually licking that part of the body with your tongue.

(4.) When you are comfortable with kissing, touching with your tongue, and, finally, with licking, begin to suck on that part of the body. Pretend that you are sucking on a lollipop, or a grape, or an orange. Open your mouth and, with the insides of your lips and tongue, suck on that part of the body.

(5.) If you did not choose the fingers or the toes, follow numbers one through four exactly on either the fingers or the toes, whichever you choose.

(6.) If you choose the fingers in number 5, now do the toes exactly the same way, following items one through four.

(7.) Place your mouth against the fleshy part of the leg, just under the knee, and follow items one through four again.

(8.) Place your mouth just behind the knee and follow items one through four again.

(9.) Place your mouth on the *back* of the thigh and do the same.

(10.) Place your mouth on the *inside* of the thigh and do the same.

(11.) Place your mouth on the penis or vagina. (Women can begin by kissing any part of the penis, following items one through four exactly. Men can begin by kissing the outside vaginal lips, then the clitoris, and then actually penetrating the vagina with the tongue if you desire.)

This procedure should be followed exactly, very slowly and gradually. You may take weeks to complete the instructions. You may take an hour. This is individual and personal. You must be in control of the situation. Discuss your feelings with each other as often as possible.

Go at your own pace. Stop at one part of the body if you want to stop there and don't go any further. Ask your partner to help you in whatever way you feel important. One woman we know found it very helpful if her husband read pornographic literature. She found that the more excited she was the more comfortable she was when she was beginning these exercises. Many men enjoy examining the woman's vagina both visually and with their fingers before they begin the exercises. One man told me that he didn't understand what the vagina looked like, where the clitoris really was, or what he should do when he found it. His ignorance kept him from oral sex more than anything else. Other men have said that the excitement they feel just from looking at the vagina and studying it without embarrassment or restraint increases their desire to have oral sex with their partner.

Therefore, I suggest that men experience the pleasure of examining their partner's vagina as thoroughly as possible when they feel comfortable and want to. We often forget that the penis is easily accessible for visual and tactile study. Most women have done this often and naturally. But since the vagina is not so easily accessible, it is often ignored.

Use the help yourself therapy program when you are working on these inhibitions. Remember that it is the *complete* program which has helped hundreds of people. Do not use just this one chapter and expect success. *All* of the exercises are vital to your treatment.

There are many sexual activities which you may wish to try but feel inhibited about. If you want to change the situation, if you want to "open the door," you can. You can use the desensitization program to remove an inhibition against anal sex, for instance. Begin by doing something which is simple for you to do, such as kissing another part of the body as described in the oral sex program. Be patient, go slowly and gradually. If you would like to enjoy anal penetration, begin with small objects such as a small vibrator or a cocktail mixer. Next, if you find it pleasurable to be penetrated by these small objects, use your fingers. Then use the penis, if the woman enjoys the penetration and feels she would like penis penetration as well. Be sure that the woman is well lubricated if you try this. Be sure that you are at the height of the excitation too.

The many relaxation exercises, the exercises to increase communication are essential to success in this program. The contracts are essential. You must utilize all of this information. Communicate with each other, discuss what it is that you'd like to try. Relax each other before attempting any behavior. Then go about it slowly, without any pressure or demand on yourself or your partner.

You can use this desensitization program if you are inhibited about masturbation. Self-stimulation of the genitals is pleasurable, healthy and one of the inhibitions put upon us by society.

Children are told not to "do it" and warned against the horrors of "growing hair on your palms" or even "going blind." Masturbation was even considered a sign of insanity. Probably still is by some people.

The fact is that there is no physical or psychological reason why you should not masturbate. You cannot do it TOO MUCH, you cannot cause any illnesses, you cannot suffer from sexual incapacity because of it. It has, in fact, been shown that if you are free about your own body and about your masturbatory practices, you will suffer least from any sexual dysfunction.

Masturbation is one of the pleasures of sexual activity, either self-masturbation or with a partner, both of which are recommended. Many women find that masturbation is one of the only things which brings them to climax. They, of course, must use this method and should use it. It can be perfectly wonderful and exciting.

Unfortunately, we have been brought up with such restrictions and told such horror stories that many of us are inhibited against this practice. If you are, please use the techniques in the desensitization program in Chapter 19, and the masturbation exercises in Chapter 16 for females. Learn to enjoy your own body. Look in the mirror. Touch yourself ALL OVER. Realize how good YOU can be to YOU. Make masturbation a beautiful word. Give it the place it deserves.

At this point, I'd like to share some of my personal inhibitions with you. Perhaps these desensitization techniques could be used to help you participate in activities which I personally oppose. But I certainly don't suggest it since I strongly oppose group sex, bestiality and sadomasochism. In my opinion, certain sexual behavior is unhealthy and because of this is without pleasure and joy.

Group sex is one such area. I feel it is highly depersonalized, dehumanizing, goal-oriented and mechanistic. All of the activities which I've read about, observed, and heard about from my patients reinforce my feelings. The emotional effects are debilitating and often sad.

Bestiality is another practice I do not approve of. I feel strongly that sex with animals is extremely dangerous. There is a strong possibility of infection. There is also the very good possibility that an animal may lose control and cause serious damage. One woman I know had been practicing bestiality with her Labrador retriever. The dog had been satisfactorily licking the woman's genital area for more than one year. One day, for no apparent reason, the dog bit the woman's labia. She almost died from loss of blood and required surgery which caused considerable pain. Many women have gotten internal infections from dogs after penetration. Because of the possibility of danger to health, bestiality is not an experience I would like to be awakened to.

Another sexual practice which I am opposed to is sadomasochism. I don't consider any form of pain—no matter how slight—to have any connection with joy and pleasure. The desire to experience pain, fear, subjugation, etc., during the sex act is one that is foreign to me and one which I don't care to have.

I am not talking about someone who likes being kissed very hard, or even bitten lightly on the body during sexual foreplay. I'm not discussing a slight slap on the behind or the game-playing of fulfilling each other's fantasy by pretending to be raped, kidnapped, or enslaved. I am discussing the pain-inflicting practices of sadomasochists who use various tools and instruments and actually enjoy giving and receiving pain.

I also feel that if you do enjoy bestiality or sadomasochism, you should consider seeing a psychiatrist to discuss your situation. Perhaps it is all right for you, and not a serious problem. If so, you'll find this out after one or two sessions with the doctor. But if it is a serious problem, as most probably it is, then you should find that out and begin to get treatment.

My feelings on these subjects are my own. I share them with you at this point because I feel strongly about them and because I want to be very certain that no one thinks that this program can succeed for persons with such serious problems.

You Can Be Your Own Sex Therapist is a help-yourself-therapy program which I have developed and found to be successful with persons who were essentially healthy. They had sexual dysfunctions, inhibitions which were given them by social pressure, inabilities to enjoy sex as fully as they wanted to and feelings of inadequacy due to sexual failure. They were not psychologically or physically ill. Persons who are psychologically or physically ill must seek the proper professional help.

You Can Be Your Own Sex Therapist is a systematic, behavioral approach to enhancing your sexual life and curing your sexual inabilities—if you have any. This chapter has been devoted to shedding inhibitions which you feel are curtailing the joy you get out of your sexual life. Decide for yourself if you have an inhibition you want to overcome. Then follow the procedures outlined.

If you have now read this book for the first time, and understand the principles and exercises that make help yourself therapy succeed, you are now ready to read the book again and go to work. Following the program I've developed, you should be able to open any door you choose to.

I'm glad you're involved in growth and change. I'm glad to have a part in it. But, remember, this program is yours. The choices are yours. Success is yours. . . .

Section V

ADDENDUM

ADDENDUM

We've come full circle. From orgasm to impotence; from the ecstasy of fulfilling sex to the agony of sexual failures; from frustration to satisfaction; and from the joy of finding your sexual self to the sadness, yet excitement of the search. We've known the extrinsic pleasures of the sexual revolution of the 60's, 70's and 80's, and we've come to recognize the internal emotional pains and emptiness of so-called "free sex." And - we've come to the era of AIDS. The dreaded Acquired Immune Deficiency Syndrome which has killed 343,000 human beings since its' onset in 1981.

The sexual revolution came to a sudden and halting stop for many reasons, but the most driving and motivating force behind this, is the fear of AIDS. Briefly allow me to expand upon the awareness that multiple partners, meaningless and transient sex, however momentarily satisfying, was wearing thin on our emotional and psychological needs. As human beings, the sexual urge has multiple components. However strong and prevalent the physical urge may be, the emotional needs are as pervasive and influential. The sexual revolution did not fulfill these needs. In fact the pressure on many to engage in frequent and unconnected sex, seemed to deteriorate and weaken emotional states. Many men and women, realizing the emptiness of "free sex," and the truth that there is no "free" anything were becoming more involved in the big C, commitment, and the big A, abstinence. Even as early as the 1970's, I was seeing young men, apparently healthy in every way, who were complaining about impotence. These young

men were "situationally" impotent. They were attempting to
engage in sex with women in whom they were not interested.
Some young men reported that there was an unpleasant odor,
or abrasive behavior, or an unclean apartment, among other
turn-offs. Yet they felt obligated to "perform" since the women
had indicated desire. The bodies of these young men were
refusing to do what their minds did not do. Their bodies were
saying "NO", responding to their hearts. But, when they failed
to become erect and perform, they feared impotence. This is
just a small example of the negative results of the pressures
and dissatisfactions of the sexual revolution. Women were
following the dictates of the "times," but their hearts were hurt
and their bodies unfulfilled. The realization that we are a
complete and complex animal, with multiple needs has
become clearer with the advent of sex therapy as it is practiced
today, even more so than in the past. Today, we recognize that
the orgasm, a response to a variety of physiological
experiences as explained elsewhere in this book, is not
complete without the emotional component, so essential to the
satisfaction and pleasure of the orgasm. Love is not the
operative word, but connection certainly is. Without the
emotional safety of connection and involvement, the orgasm is
momentary, fleeting, and the aftermath often empty, even
painful. With realization and recognition of the complexity of
the sexual experience, and our complex needs which must be
fulfilled, sex therapy approaches all clients as a gestalt, a
whole person. The techniques and practices are the same, as in
the chapters herewith. However, I feel obligated to recognize
that I may have failed to stress emotional aspects of human
sexuality as much as I wanted to, and want to remind you that
YOU and YOUR needs will be satisfied when practicing these
techniques, doing this homework, and learning to overcome
YOUR problems. Do not go beyond your own wishes and
needs. Do not go beyond your own emotional abilities or
requirements. Your sex life is exactly that - YOURS. Do not
sacrifice to another person if it feels like sacrifice. Do only
what is comfortable and is necessary so that your happiness is

fulfilled. Do not do what is uncomfortable or not for your own pleasures. I say this now, and I say this strongly because of the grave situation in which we find ourselves Sexual satisfaction and the fulfilling of any sexual drive must be tempered with our own needs and desires, our own sense of safety, and our own protective mechanisms. We must not be victims to the demands of others. AIDS is the driving force of this new determination.

A History of Aids

In 1981, five otherwise healthy young men were diagnosed with Pneumocystis carunii pneumonia. This particular form of pneumonia was associated with a severe depression of the immune system.

Due to the brilliance and insight of doctors treating these men, a report was filed and the search was on for the cause of this "problem." AIDS was the answer. Due to the diligence of the Center for Disease Control, by the end of 1982 a common cause was discovered. The agent affecting the immune system seemed to be transmitted sexually in men, and later learned to be carried in the blood stream thus forcing the demand that the blood supply be protected from this unknown agent. Within 21 months of the first five cases reported, the HIV Human Immunodeficiency Virus was isolated and reported as the cause of AIDS. Since then, there has been some controversy regarding this, but it is still widely believed that HIV is the direct cause of AIDS. The next step was to discover where and how the HIV is transmitted. These are the facts:

HIV is transmitted through sexual fluids: semen, vaginal secretions, blood, saliva, and tears. However, exposure to saliva and tears infected with HIV has not been proven to transmit the infection, unless the fluid goes directly into the blood stream. This scenario would be highly unusual. Unless there is an open and bleeding sore in the mouth, or other area which saliva or tears contacted.

It is also true that all evidence indicates that non-sexual but close contact with infected patients does NOT appear to be a threat if precautions are taken. Aids is not transmitted through the skin or pores, through mosquitoes, or utensils, or foods, or dishes.

High risk groups:

> Sexually active gay and bi-sexual men and their female partners.

> Intravenous drug users and their partners.

> Those requiring blood transmissions, especially prior to 1986 when the blood banks were more carefully screened.

> Immigrants - especially Thailand, East and Central African and Haiti where AIDS is seriously rampant.

PLEASE:

If you do not know your prospective sexual partner, abstain until a test can be conducted. Keep in mind that the HIV can be dormant for as many as six months, so that a negative test is not necessarily safe.

If you do not abstain, practice safe sex:

> Mutual masturbation, only if you do not have any opens sores through which semen or vaginal secretions could pass directly into your blood stream.

> Avoid anal sex.

> Oral sex if you do not allow the semen to enter your

mouth. Stimulate only the vaginal lips so that vaginal secretions do not enter your mouth.

Ancillary Sex: Stimulation of the erogenous zones with fingers, rubbing of body parts between breasts, under the arms, between the thighs, etc.

ALWAYS use a LATEX condom if you do engage in penile-vaginal penetration. Unless you are absolutely sure that your partner is NOT infected.

ALWAYS avoid any sexual contact during which a sexual secretion can enter an open sore, or any opening which may go directly to your blood stream.

Do Not allow this epidemic to cause you to avoid all sexual contact and pleasure. But, please, do be careful.

"You Can Be Your Own Sex Therapist"

You can create a more exciting and fulfilling sex life than you are now experiencing. I wrote this book for YOU, so that You can learn new techniques, broaden your sexual horizons, and look towards healthier and more complete experiences. I wish you health, sensuality, and sexuality in all that you do. I wish you love.

Index